A G I F T F O R :

....

F R O M :

....

Published by J Countryman, a division of Thomas Nelson, Inc., Nashville, Tennessee, 37214.

Compiled and edited by Terri Gibbs.

Design by The DesignWorks Group, www.thedesignworksgroup.com;
        cover, Wes Youssi; interior, Robin Black.

ISBN: 1-4041-0378-3

www.thomasnelson.com
www.jcountryman.com

Printed and bound in Belgium.

GOD'S
PROMISES®
for YOU

SCRIPTURE SELECTIONS FROM
MAX LUCADO

A Division of Thomas Nelson Publishers
Since 1798
www.thomasnelson.com

FOREWORD

Do you believe God is near? He wants you to. He wants you to know he is in the midst of your world. Wherever you are, he is present. In your car. On the plane. In your office, your bedroom, your den. He's near.

He's involved in the car pools, heartbreaks, and funeral homes of our day. He is as near to us on Monday as on Sunday. In the school room as in the sanctuary. At the coffee break as much as the communion table.

That is why his Word speaks to the things in our world. It is not addressed to aliens in a distant galaxy. It is addressed to you and me. It speaks to our needs, our hopes, our dreams.

Wherever you are in life, wherever you go in this world, I pray this little book of God's promises will remind you that he is always near. As you read, may you find that his promises speak of his personal passion for you.

His faithfulness is clear. His will to change the world, relentless.

He has drawn near to you.

MAX LUCADO

PROMISES
to
GIVE INSIGHT

PROMISES ABOUT LOVE

Love is patient and kind. Love is not jealous,
it does not brag, and it is not proud. Love is not rude,
is not selfish, and does not get upset with others.
Love does not count up wrongs that have been done.
Love is not happy with evil but is happy with the truth.
Love patiently accepts all things. It always trusts,
always hopes, and always remains strong.

1 CORINTHIANS 13:4–7

We know the love that God has for us,
and we trust that love. God is love.
Those who live in love live in God,
and God lives in them.

1 JOHN 4:16

The Father himself loves you. He loves you
because you loved me and believed that I came from God.

JOHN 16:27

I give you a new command: Love each other.
You must love each other as I have loved you.
All people will know that you are my followers
if you love each other.

JOHN 13:34–35

LOVE

Our love depends on the receiver of the love. Let a thousand people pass before us, and we will not feel the same about each. Our love will be regulated by their appearance, by their personalities. Even when we find a few people we like, our feelings will fluctuate. How they treat us will affect how we love them. The receiver regulates our love.

Not so with the love of God. We have no thermostatic impact on his love for us. The love of God is born from within him, not from what he finds in us. His love is uncaused and spontaneous.

Does he love us because of our goodness? Because of our kindness? Because of our great faith? No, he loves us because of *his* goodness, kindness, and great faith.

A Love Worth Giving

9

PROMISES ABOUT FAITH

Faith means being sure of the things we hope for and knowing that something is real even if we do not see it. . . . It is by faith we understand that the whole world was made by God's command so what we see was made by something that cannot be seen. . . . Without faith no one can please God. Anyone who comes to God must believe that he is real and that he rewards those who truly want to find him.

HEBREWS 11:1, 3, 6

The Good News shows how God makes people right with himself—that it begins and ends with faith. As the Scripture says, "But those who are right with God will live by trusting in him."

ROMANS 1:17

We have troubles all around us, but we are not defeated. We do not know what to do, but we do not give up the hope of living. We are persecuted, but God does not leave us. We are hurt sometimes, but we are not destroyed. . . . So we do not give up. Our physical body is becoming older and weaker, but our spirit inside us is made new every day. We have small troubles for a while now, but they are helping us gain an eternal glory that is much greater than the troubles. We set our eyes not on what we see but on what we cannot see. . . .

2 CORINTHIANS 4:8–9, 16–18

FAITH

Faith is the belief that God is real and that God is good. . . . It is a choice to believe that the one who made it all hasn't left it all and that he still sends light into the shadows and responds to gestures of faith. . . .

Faith is the belief that God will do what is right.

God says that the more hopeless your circumstances, the more likely your salvation. The greater your cares, the more genuine your prayers. The darker the room, the greater the need for light.

God's help is near and always available, but it is only given to those who seek it.

HE STILL MOVES STONES

PROMISES ABOUT CONTENTMENT

Serving God does make us very rich, if we are satisfied with what we have. We brought nothing into the world, so we can take nothing out. But, if we have food and clothes, we will be satisfied with that. Those who want to become rich bring temptation to themselves and are caught in a trap. They want many foolish and harmful things that ruin and destroy people. The love of money causes all kinds of evil. Some people have left the faith, because they wanted to get more money, but they have caused themselves much sorrow.

1 TIMOTHY 6:6–10

Do not worry about anything, but pray and ask God for everything you need, always giving thanks. And God's peace, which is so great we cannot understand it, will keep your hearts and minds in Christ Jesus. . . . I have learned to be satisfied with the things I have and with everything that happens. I know how to live when I am poor, and I know how to live when I have plenty. I have learned the secret of being happy at any time in everything that happens. . . . I can do all things through Christ, because he gives me strength.

PHILIPPIANS 4:6–7, 11–13

CONTENTMENT

Satisfied? That is one thing we are not. We are not satisfied. . . .

We take a vacation of a lifetime. . . . We satiate ourselves with sun, fun, and good food. But we are not even on the way home before we dread the end of the trip and begin planning another.

We are not satisfied.

As a child we say, "If only I were a teenager." As a teen we say, "If only I were an adult." As an adult, "If only I were married." As a spouse, "If only I had kids." . . .

We are not satisfied. Contentment is a difficult virtue. Why?

Because there is nothing on earth that can satisfy our deepest longing. We long to see God. The leaves of life are rustling with the rumor that we will— and we won't be satisfied until we do.

WHEN GOD WHISPERS YOUR NAME

No king is saved by his great army.
No warrior escapes by his great strength. . . .
But the LORD looks after those who fear him,
those who put their hope in his love.
He saves them from death
and spares their lives in times of hunger.
So our hope is in the LORD.
He is our help, our shield to protect us.

PSALM 33:16, 18–20

If God is with us, no one can defeat us.
He did not spare his own Son but gave him for us all.
So with Jesus, God will surely give us all things.
Who can accuse the people God has chosen?
No one, because God is the One who makes them right.

ROMANS 8:31–33

The LORD's love never ends;
his mercies never stop.
They are new every morning;
LORD , your loyalty is great.
I say to myself, "The LORD is mine,
so I hope in him."
The LORD is good to those who hope in him,
to those who seek him.

LAMENTATIONS 3:22–25

HOPE

It's hard to see things grow old. The town in which I grew up is growing old. . . . Some of the buildings are boarded up. Some of the houses are torn down. . . . The old movie house where I took my dates has "For Sale" on the marquee. . . .

I wish I could make it all new again. I wish I could blow the dust off the streets . . . but I can't.

I can't. But God can. "He restores my soul," wrote the shepherd. He doesn't reform; he restores. He doesn't camouflage the old; he restores the new. The Master Builder will pull out the original plan and restore it. He will restore the vigor. He will restore the energy. He will restore the hope. He will restore the soul.

THE APPLAUSE OF HEAVEN

The teachings of the LORD are perfect;
they give new strength.
The rules of the LORD can be trusted;
they make plain people wise. . . .
The judgments of the LORD are true;
they are completely right.

PSALM 19:7–9

How I love your teachings!
I think about them all day long.
Your commands make me wiser than my enemies,
because they are mine forever. . . .
Your words are true from the start,
and all your laws will be fair forever.

PSALM 119:97, 98, 160

We also know that the Son of God has come
and has given us understanding so that we can know
the True One. And our lives are in the True One and in
his Son, Jesus Christ.
He is the true God and the eternal life.

1 JOHN 5:20

TRUTH

Imagine that you are an ice skater in competition. You are in first place with one more round to go. If you perform well, the trophy is yours. You are nervous, anxious, and frightened.

Then, only minutes before your performance, your trainer rushes to you with the thrilling news: "You've already won! The judges tabulated the scores, and the person in second place can't catch you. You are too far ahead."

Upon hearing that news, how will you feel? Exhilarated!

And how will you skate? . . . How about courageously and confidently? You bet you will. You will do your best because the prize is yours.

The point is clear: the truth will triumph. The Father of truth will win, and the followers of truth will be saved.

THE APPLAUSE OF HEAVEN

17

PROMISES ABOUT
STRENGTH

He gives strength to those who are tired
and more power to those who are weak.
The people who trust the LORD will
become strong again.
They will rise up as an eagle in the sky;
they will run and not need rest;
they will walk and not become tired.

ISAIAH 40:29, 31

Come to me, all of you who are tired and
have heavy loads, and I will give you rest.
Accept my teachings and learn from me,
because I am gentle and humble in spirit,
and you will find rest for your lives.
The teaching that I ask you to accept is easy;
the load I give you to carry is light.

MATTHEW 11:28–30

God is our protection and our strength.
He always helps in times of trouble.
The LORD All-Powerful is with us;
the God of Jacob is our defender.

PSALM 46:1, 11

STRENGTH

An example of faith was found on the wall of a concentration camp. On it a prisoner had carved the words:

I believe in the sun, even though it doesn't shine,
I believe in love, even when it isn't shown,
I believe in God, even when he doesn't speak.

I try to imagine the person who etched those words. I try to envision his skeletal hand gripping the broken glass or stone that cut into the wall. I try to imagine his eyes squinting through the darkness as he carved each letter. What hand could have cut such a conviction? What eyes could have seen good in such horror?

There is only one answer: Eyes that chose to see the unseen.

HE STILL MOVES STONES

PROMISES ABOUT PATIENCE

We also have joy with our troubles,
because we know that these troubles produce patience.
And patience produces character, and character produces hope.
And this hope will never disappoint us, because God
has poured out his love to fill our hearts.

ROMANS 5:3–5

We have around us many people whose lives tell us
what faith means. So let us run the race that is before us
and never give up. We should remove from our lives anything
that would get in the way and the sin that so easily
holds us back. Let us look only to Jesus, the One who
began our faith and who makes it perfect.

HEBREWS 12:1–2A

My brothers and sisters, when you have many
kinds of troubles, you should be full of joy, because you
know that these troubles test your faith, and this will give
you patience. Let your patience show itself perfectly in
what you do. Then you will be perfect and complete
and will have everything you need.

JAMES 1:2–4

PATIENCE

God is often more patient with us than we are with ourselves. We assume that if we fall, we aren't born again. If we stumble, then we aren't truly converted. If we have the old desires, then we must not be a new creation.

If you are anxious about this, please remember, "God began doing a good work in you, and I am sure he will continue it until it is finished when Jesus Christ comes again" (Philippians 1:6).

A GENTLE THUNDER

PROMISES
About God

PROMISES ABOUT
GOD'S LOVE

This is what real love is:
It is not our love for God; it is God's love
for us in sending his Son
to be the way to take away our sins.

1 JOHN 4:10

The LORD did not care for you and choose you
because there were many of you—you are the smallest
nation of all. But the LORD chose you because
he loved you and kept his promise to your ancestors.

DEUTERONOMY 7:7–8

Love never ends.
These three things continue forever:
faith, hope, and love.
And the greatest of these is love.

1 CORINTHIANS 13:8, 13

GOD'S LOVE

God's love does not hinge on yours. The abundance of your love does not increase his. The lack of your love does not diminish his. Your goodness does not enhance his love, nor does your weakness dilute it.

God loves you simply because he has chosen to do so.

He loves you when you don't feel lovely.

He loves you when no one else loves you.

Others may abandon you, divorce you, and ignore you, but God will love you. Always. No matter what.

A LOVE WORTH GIVING

PROMISES ABOUT
GOD'S MERCY

The LORD passed in front of Moses and said,
"I am the LORD. The LORD is a God who shows mercy,
who is kind, who doesn't become angry quickly,
who has great love and faithfulness
and is kind to thousands of people."

EXODUS 34:6–7A

God will show his mercy forever and ever
to those who worship and serve him.

LUKE 1:50

But God's mercy is great, and he loved us very much.
Though we were spiritually dead because of the things
we did against God, he gave us new life with Christ.
You have been saved by God's grace.

EPHESIANS 2:4–5

GOD'S MERCY

God does not save us because of what we've done. Only a puny god could be bought with tithes. Only an egotistical god would be impressed with our pain. Only a temperamental god could be satisfied by sacrifices. Only a heartless god would sell salvation to the highest bidders.

And only a great God does for his children what they can't do for themselves.

God's delight is received upon surrender, not awarded upon conquest. The first step to joy is a plea for help, an acknowledgment of moral destitution, an admission of inward paucity. Those who taste God's presence have declared spiritual bankruptcy and are aware of their spiritual crisis. . . . Their pockets are empty. Their options are gone. They have long since stopped demanding justice; they are pleading for mercy.

THE APPLAUSE OF HEAVEN

PROMISES ABOUT GOD'S FAITHFULNESS

I will always sing about the LORD's love;
I will tell of his loyalty from now on.
I will say, "Your love continues forever;
your loyalty goes on and on like the sky."

PSALM 89:1–2

So know that the LORD your God is God,
the faithful God. He will keep his agreement
of love for a thousand lifetimes for people who
love him and obey his commands.

DEUTERONOMY 7:9

Jesus will keep you strong until the end
so that there will be no wrong in you on the day
our Lord Jesus Christ comes again. God, who has
called you to share everything with his Son,
Jesus Christ our Lord, is faithful.

1 CORINTHIANS 1:8–9

GOD'S FAITHFULNESS

We are God's idea. We are his. His face. His eyes. His hands. His touch. We are him. Look deeply into the face of every human being on earth, and you will see his likeness. Though some appear to be distant relatives, they are not. God has no cousins, only children.

We are incredibly, the body of Christ. And though we may not act like our Father, there is no greater truth than this: We are his. Unalterably. He loves us. Undyingly. Nothing can separate us from the love of Christ (see Romans 8:38–39).

A GENTLE THUNDER

PROMISES ABOUT
GOD'S STEADFASTNESS

There is no God like you.
You forgive those who are guilty of sin. . . .
You will not stay angry forever,
because you enjoy being kind.
You will have mercy on us.

MICAH 7:18–19

Every word of God is true.
He guards those who come to him for safety.

PROVERBS 30:5

The LORD is kind and shows mercy.
He does not become angry quickly but is full of love.
The LORD is good to everyone;
he is merciful to all he has made.

PSALM 145:8–9

GOD'S STEADFASTNESS

God never gives up.

When Joseph was dropped into a pit by his own brothers, God didn't give up.

When Moses said, "Here I am, send Aaron," God didn't give up. . . .

When the delivered Israelites wanted Egyptian slavery instead of milk and honey, God didn't give up.

When Samson whispered to Delilah, when Saul roared after David, when David schemed against Uriah, God didn't give up.

When Peter worshiped Him at the supper and cursed Him at the fire, He didn't give up.

God never gives up.

SIX HOURS ONE FRIDAY

PROMISES ABOUT
GOD'S COMFORT

The LORD hears good people when they cry out to him,
and he saves them from all their troubles.
The LORD is close to the brokenhearted,
and he saves those whose spirits have been crushed.

PSALM 34:17–18

God is the Father who is full of mercy and all comfort.
He comforts us every time we have trouble,
so when others have trouble, we can comfort them
with the same comfort God gives us. We share in
the many sufferings of Christ. In the same way,
much comfort comes to us through Christ.

2 CORINTHIANS 1:3–5

Even if I walk through a very dark valley,
I will not be afraid, because you are with me.
Your rod and your walking stick comfort me.

PSALM 23:4

GOD'S COMFORT

There are historical moments in which a real God met real pain so we could answer the question, "Where is God when I hurt?"

How does God react to dashed hopes? Read the story of Jairus. How does the Father feel about those who are ill? Stand with him at the pool of Bethesda. Do you long for God to speak to your lonely heart? Then listen as he speaks to the Emmaus-bound disciples. . . .

He's not doing it just for them. He's doing it for me. He's doing it for you. . . .

The God who spoke still speaks. . . . The God who came still comes. He comes into our world. He comes into your world. He comes to do what you can't.

HE STILL MOVES STONES

PROMISES ABOUT
GOD'S BLESSINGS

*Praise be to the God and Father of our Lord Jesus Christ.
In Christ, God has given us every spiritual blessing
in the heavenly world. That is, in Christ, he chose us
before the world was made so that we would be
his holy people—people without blame before him.*

EPHESIANS 1:3–4

*The same Lord is the Lord of all and gives many
blessings to all who trust in him, as the Scripture says,
"Anyone who calls on the Lord will be saved."*

ROMANS 10:12–13

*Every good action and every perfect gift is
from God. These good gifts come down from
the Creator of the sun, moon, and stars,
who does not change like their shifting shadows.*

JAMES 1:17

GOD'S BLESSINGS

To recognize God as Lord is to acknowledge that he is sovereign and supreme in the universe. To accept him as Savior is to accept his gift of salvation offered on the cross. To regard him as Father is to go a step further. Ideally, a father is the one in your life who provides and protects. This is exactly what God has done.

He has provided for your needs (Matthew 6:25–34). He has protected you from harm (Psalm 139:5). He has adopted you (Ephesians 1:5). And he has given you his name (1 John 3:1).

God has proven himself as a faithful father. Now it falls to us to be trusting children.

He Still Moves Stones

PROMISES ABOUT
GOD'S GUIDANCE

The LORD will always lead you.
He will satisfy your needs in dry lands
and give strength to your bones.
You will be like a garden that has much water,
like a spring that never runs dry.

ISAIAH 58:11

People make plans in their minds,
but only the LORD can make them come true.
Depend on the LORD in whatever you do,
and your plans will succeed.

PROVERBS 16:1, 3

Do not change yourselves to be like the people
of this world, but be changed within by a new way
of thinking. Then you will be able to decide what God
wants for you; you will know what is good
and pleasing to him and what is perfect.

ROMANS 12:2

GOD'S GUIDANCE

You've been there. You've escaped the sandy foundations of the valley and ascended his grand outcropping of granite. You've turned your back on the noise and sought his voice. You've stepped away from the masses and followed the Master as he led you up the winding path to the summit. . . .

Gently your guide invites you to sit on the rock above the tree line and look out with him at the ancient peaks that will never erode. "What is necessary is still what is sure," he confides. "Just remember:

You'll go nowhere tomorrow that I haven't already been.

Truth will still triumph. . . .

The victory is yours. . . ."

The sacred summit. A place of permanence in a world of transition.

THE APPLAUSE OF HEAVEN

PROMISES ABOUT
GOD'S GRACE

Our high priest is able to understand our weaknesses.
When he lived on earth, he was tempted in every way that
we are, but he did not sin. Let us, then, feel very sure
that we can come before God's throne where there is grace.
There we can receive mercy and grace to help us
when we need it.

HEBREWS 4:15–16

You have been saved by grace through believing.
You did not save yourselves; it was a gift from God.
It was not the result of your own efforts,
so you cannot brag about it.

EPHESIANS 2:8–9

And after you suffer for a short time, God,
who gives all grace, will make everything right.
He will make you strong and support you and
keep you from falling. He called you to share in his
glory in Christ, a glory that will continue forever.

1 PETER 5:10

GOD'S GRACE

You may be decent. You may pay taxes and kiss your kids and sleep with a clean conscience. But apart from Christ you aren't holy. So how can you go to heaven?

Only believe. Accept the work already done, the work of Jesus on the cross.

Accept the goodness of Jesus Christ. Abandon your own works and accept his. Abandon your own decency and accept his. Stand before God in his name, not yours.

It's that easy? There was nothing easy about it at all. The cross was heavy, the blood was real, and the price was extravagant. It would have bankrupted you or me, so he paid it for us. Call it simple. Call it a gift. But don't call it easy.

Call it what it is. Call it grace.

A Gentle Thunder

PROMISES ABOUT GOD'S POWER

When a believing person prays,
great things happen.

JAMES 5:16

With God's power working in us,
God can do much,
much more than anything
we can ask or imagine.

EPHESIANS 3:20

I tell you to believe
that you have received the things
you ask for in prayer,
and God will give them to you.

MARK 11:24

GOD'S POWER

"If you believe, you will get anything you ask for in prayer." (Matthew 21:22)

Don't reduce this grand statement to the category of new cars and paychecks. Don't limit the promise of this passage to the selfish pool of perks and favors. The fruit God assures is far greater than earthly wealth. His dreams are much greater than promotions and proposals.

God wants you to fly. He wants you to fly free of yesterday's guilt. He wants you to fly free of today's fears. He wants you to fly free of tomorrow's grave. Sin, fear, and death. These are the mountains he has moved. These are the prayers he will answer.

AND THE ANGELS WERE SILENT

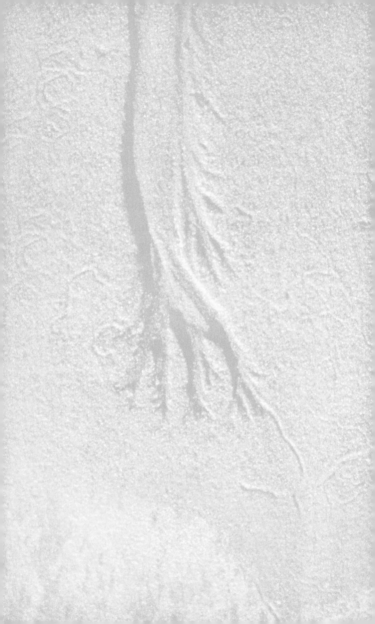

PROMISES
About
CHRISTIAN LIVING

PROMISES ABOUT
SERVING GOD

In all the work you are doing,
work the best you can. Work as if you were doing it
for the Lord, not for people. Remember that you
will receive your reward from the Lord, which he
promised to his people. You are serving the Lord Christ.

COLOSSIANS 3:23–24

Then Jesus called the crowd to him,
along with his followers. He said, "If people want
to follow me, they must give up the things they want.
They must be willing even to give up their lives
to follow me. Those who want to save their lives
will give up true life. But those who give up their lives
for me and for the Good News will have true life."

MARK 8:34–35

The servant does not get any special thanks
for doing what his master commanded. It is the same
with you. When you have done everything you are
told to do, you should say, "We are unworthy servants;
we have only done the work we should do."

LUKE 17:9–10

SERVING GOD

On one side stands the crowd.

Jeering. Baiting. Demanding.

On the other stands a peasant.

Swollen lips. Lumpy eye. Lofty promise.

One promises acceptance,

the other a cross.

One offers flesh and flash,

the other offers faith.

The crowd challenges, "Follow us and fit in."

Jesus promises, "Follow me and stand out."

They promise to please.

God promises to save.

God looks at you and asks . . .

"Which will be your choice?"

A GENTLE THUNDER

PROMISES ABOUT
PRAISING GOD

Praise the LORD for the glory of his name;
worship the LORD because he is holy.

PSALM 29:2

Sing praises to the LORD, you who belong to him;
praise his holy name.

PSALM 30:4

Come, let's worship him and bow down.
Let's kneel before the LORD who made us,
because he is our God
and we are the people he takes care of
and the sheep that he tends.

PSALM 95:6–7

Praise the LORD!
Praise God in his Temple;
praise him in his mighty heaven.
Praise him for his strength;
praise him for his greatness.
Let everything that breathes praise the LORD.
Praise the LORD!

PSALM 150:1–2, 6

PRAISING GOD

From where I write I can see several miracles. White-crested waves slap the beach with rhythmic regularity. One after the other the rising swells of salt water gain momentum, humping, rising, then standing to salute the beach before crashing onto the sand.

In the distance lies a miracle of colors—twins of blue. The ocean-blue of the Atlantic encounters the pale blue of the sky, separated only by the horizon, stretched like a taut wire between two poles.

It is the normality not the uniqueness of God's miracles that causes them to be so staggering. Rather than shocking the globe with an occasional demonstration of deity, God has opted to display his power daily. Proverbially. Pounding waves. Prism-cast colors. Birth, death, life. We are surrounded by miracles. God is throwing testimonies at us like fireworks, each one exploding, "God is! God is!"

GOD CAME NEAR

PROMISES ABOUT GIVING TO GOD

Honor the LORD with your wealth
and the firstfruits from all your crops.
Then your barns will be full,
and your wine barrels will overflow with new wine.

PROVERBS 3:9–10

Bring to the storehouse a full tenth
of what you earn so there will be food in my house.
Test me in this. . . . I will open the windows of heaven
for you and pour out all the blessings you need.

MALACHI 3:10

Give, and you will receive. You will be given much.
Pressed down, shaken together, and running over,
it will spill into your lap. The way you give
to others is the way God will give to you.

LUKE 6:38

GIVING TO GOD

"Blessed are the meek," Jesus explained. Blessed are the available. Blessed are the conduits, the tunnels, the tools. Deliriously joyful are the ones who believe that if God has used sticks, rocks, and spit to do his will, then he can use us. . . .

A small cathedral outside Bethlehem marks the supposed birthplace of Jesus. Behind a high altar in the church is a cave, a little cavern lit by silver lamps.

You can enter the main edifice and admire the ancient church. You can also enter the quiet cave where a star embedded in the floor recognizes the birth of the King. There is one stipulation, however. You have to stoop. The door is so low you can't go in standing up. . . .

You can see the world standing tall, but to witness the Savior, you have to get on your knees.

THE APPLAUSE OF HEAVEN

PROMISES ABOUT
READING GOD'S WORD

God's word is alive and working
and is sharper than a double-edged sword.
It cuts all the way into us, where the soul and
the spirit are joined, to the center of our joints and bones.
And it judges the thoughts and feelings in our hearts.

HEBREWS 4:12

The truly happy people are those who
carefully study God's perfect law that makes people free,
and they continue to study it. They do not forget
what they heard, but they obey what God's teaching says.
Those who do this will be made happy.

JAMES 1:25

As newborn babies want milk,
you should want the pure and simple teaching.
By it you can grow up and be saved, because you have
already examined and seen how good the Lord is.

1 PETER 2:2

READING GOD'S WORD

The Bible has been banned, burned, scoffed, and ridiculed. Scholars have mocked it as foolish. Kings have branded it as illegal. A thousand times over it the grave has been dug and the dirge has begun, but somehow the Bible never stays in the grave. Not only has it survived, it has thrived. It is the single most popular book in all of history. It has been the best-selling book in the world for years!

There is no way on earth to explain it. Which perhaps is the only explanation. The answer? The Bible's durability is not found on earth; it is found in heaven. For the millions who have tested its claims and claimed its promises there is but one answer—the Bible is God's book and God's voice.

THE INSPIRATIONAL STUDY BIBLE

PROMISES ABOUT
OBEYING GOD

I have obeyed my Father's commands,
and I remain in his love. In the same way,
if you obey my commands, you will remain in my love.
I have told you these things so that you can have the same joy
I have and so that your joy will be the fullest possible joy.

JOHN 15:10–11

I will show you what everyone is like who
comes to me and hears my words and obeys.
That person is like a man building a house who dug deep
and laid the foundation on rock. When the floods came,
the water tried to wash the house away, but it could not
shake it, because the house was built well.

LUKE 6:47–48

We can be sure that we know God if we obey
his commands. Anyone who says, "I know God,"
but does not obey God's commands is a liar, and the truth
is not in that person. But if someone obeys God's teaching,
then in that person God's love has truly reached its goal.

1 JOHN 2:3–5

OBEYING GOD

Compared to God's part, our part is minuscule but necessary. We don't have to do much, *but we do have to do something.*

Write a letter.

Ask forgiveness.

Call a counselor.

Confess.

Call mom.

Visit a doctor.

Be baptized.

Feed a hungry person.

Pray.

Teach.

Go.

Do something that demonstrates faith. For faith with no effort is no faith at all.

HE STILL MOVES STONES

PROMISES ABOUT
PRAYING TO GOD

*So I tell you to believe that you have received
the things you ask for in prayer, and God will give
them to you. When you are praying, if you are angry
with someone, forgive him so that your Father in heaven
will also forgive your sins.*

MARK 11:24–25

*If my people, who are called by my name,
are sorry for what they have done, if they pray and
obey me and stop their evil ways, I will hear them
from heaven. I will forgive their sin,
and I will heal their land.*

2 CHRONICLES 7:14

*The LORD sees the good people
and listens to their prayers.
But the LORD is against those who do evil;
he makes the world forget them.*

PSALM 34:15–16

PRAYING TO GOD

"Continue earnestly in prayer, being vigilant in it with thanksgiving" (Colossians 4:2, NKJV).

Sound burdensome? Are you wondering, *My business needs attention, my children need dinner, my bills need paying. How can I stay in a place of prayer?* Unceasing prayer may sound complicated, but it needn't be that way.

Do this. Change your definition of prayer. Think of prayers less as an activity for God and more as an awareness of God. Seek to live in uninterrupted awareness. Acknowledge his presence everywhere you go. As you stand in line to register your car, think, *Thank you, Lord, for being here.* In the grocery as you shop, *Your presence, my King, I welcome.* As you wash the dishes, worship your Maker.

COME THIRSTY

PROMISES ABOUT
LOVING GOD

If you love me, you will obey my commands.
Those who know my commands and obey them are the ones who
love me, and my Father will love those who love me.
I will love them and will show myself to them.

JOHN 14:15, 21

The most important command is this: . . .
Love the Lord your God with all your heart,
all your soul, all your mind, and all your strength.

MARK 12:29–30

We love because God first loved us. . . .
Those who do not love their brothers and sisters,
whom they have seen, cannot love God, whom they have
never seen. And God gave us this command: Those who
love God must also love their brothers and sisters.

1 JOHN 4:19–21

LOVING GOD

He placed one scoop of clay upon another until a form lay lifeless on the ground. . . .

All were silent as the Creator reached in himself and removed something yet unseen. "It's called 'choice.' The seed of choice."

Within the man, God had placed a divine seed. A seed of his *self*. The God of might had created earth's mightiest. The Creator had created, not a creature, but another creator. And the One who had chosen to love had created one who could love in return.

Now it's our choice.

IN THE EYE OF THE STORM

PROMISES ABOUT
TRUSTING GOD

We worship God through his Spirit,
and our pride is in Christ Jesus.
We do not put trust in ourselves
or anything we can do. . . .

PHILIPPIANS 3:3

But the person who trusts in the LORD
will be blessed.
The LORD will show him that he can be trusted.
He will be strong, like a tree planted near water
that sends its roots by a stream.
It is not afraid when the days are hot;
its leaves are always green.
It does not worry in a year when no rain comes;
it always produces fruit.

JEREMIAH 17:7–8

When I am afraid
I will trust you.
I praise God for his word.
I trust God, so I am not afraid.
What can human beings do to me?

PSALM 56:3–4

TRUSTING GOD

Many players appear on the stage of Gethsemane. Judas and his betrayal. Peter and his sword. . . . The soldiers and their weapons. And though these are crucial, they aren't instrumental. The encounter is not between Jesus and the soldiers; it is between God and Satan. Satan dares to enter yet another garden, but God stands and Satan hasn't a prayer. . . .

Satan falls in the presence of Christ. One word from his lips, and the finest army in the world collapsed.

Satan is silent in the proclamation of Christ. Not once did the enemy speak without Jesus' invitation. Before Christ, Satan has nothing to say.

Satan is powerless against the protection of Christ. . . .

When Jesus says he will keep you safe, he means it. Hell will have to get through him to get to you. Jesus is able to protect you. When he says he will get you home, he will get you home.

A GENTLE THUNDER

PROMISES ABOUT
WORSHIPING GOD

Respect the LORD your God.
You must worship him and make your promises
only in his name. Do not worship others gods
as the people around you do, because the LORD
your God is a jealous God.

DEUTERONOMY 6:13–14

Say to God, "Your works are amazing!
Because your power is great,
your enemies fall before you.
All the earth worships you
and sings praises to you.
They sing praises to your name."

PSALM 66:3–4

The time is coming when the true worshipers
will worship the Father in spirit and truth, and that
time is here already. You see, the Father too is actively seeking
such people to worship him. God is spirit, and those who
worship him must worship in spirit and truth.

JOHN 4:23–24

WORSHIPING GOD

Worship is the "thank you" that refuses to be silenced.
We have tried to make a science out of worship.
We can't do that. We can't do that any more than we
can "sell love" or "negotiate peace."

Worship is a voluntary act of gratitude offered by
the saved to the Savior, by the healed to the Healer,
and by the delivered to the Deliverer.

IN THE EYE OF THE STORM

PROMISES
of
GUIDANCE

PROMISES ABOUT
TEMPTATION

So the Lord knows how to save those
who serve him when troubles come. . . .

2 PETER 2:9

Be strong in the Lord and in his great power.
Put on the full armor of God so that you can fight
against the devil's tricks.
Our fight is not against people on earth
but against the rulers and authorities and the power
of this world's darkness, against the spiritual powers
of evil in the heavenly world.

EPHESIANS 6:10–12

If you think you are strong,
you should be careful not to fall. The only temptation
that has come to you is that which everyone has.
But you can trust God,
who will not permit you to be tempted
more than you can stand. But when you are tempted,
he will also give you a way to escape so that
you will be able to stand it.

1 CORINTHIANS 10:12–13

TEMPTATION

"Watch and pray so that you will not fall into temptation." (Mark 14:38, NIV)

"Watch." They don't come any more practical than that. Watch. Stay alert. Keep your eyes open. When you see sin coming, duck. When you anticipate an awkward encounter, turn around. When you sense temptation, go the other way.

All Jesus is saying is, "Pay attention." You know your weaknesses. You also know the situations in which your weaknesses are most vulnerable. *Stay out of those situations.* Back seats. Late hours. Night clubs. Poker games. Bridge parties. Movie theaters. Whatever it is that gives Satan a foothold in your life, stay away from it. Watch out!

NO WONDER THEY CALL HIM THE SAVIOR

PROMISES ABOUT GUILT

*If anyone belongs to Christ, there is a new creation.
The old things have gone; everything is made new!*

2 CORINTHIANS 5:17

*So now, those who are in
Christ Jesus are not judged guilty.*

ROMANS 8:1

*When you were spiritually dead because of your sins
and because you were not free from the power of your
sinful self, God made you alive with Christ, and he
forgave all our sins. He canceled the debt, which listed
all the rules we failed to follow. He took away that
record with its rules and nailed it to the cross.*

COLOSSIANS 2:13–14

*I, I am the One who forgives all your sins,
for my sake;
I will not remember your sins.*

ISAIAH 43:25

GUILT

Have you been there? Have you felt the ground of conviction give way beneath your feet? The ledge crumbles, your eyes widen, and down you go. Poof!

Now what do you do? . . . When we fall, we can dismiss it. We can deny it. We can distort it. Or we can deal with it. . . .

We keep no secrets from God. Confession is not telling God what we did. He already knows. Confession is simply agreeing with God that our acts were wrong. . . .

How can God heal what we deny? . . . How can God grant us pardon when we won't admit our guilt?

Ahh, there's that word: *guilt*. Isn't that what we avoid? Guilt. Isn't that what we detest? But is guilt so bad? What does guilt imply if not that we know right from wrong, that we aspire to be better than we are. . . . That's what guilt is: a healthy regret for telling God one thing and doing another.

A GENTLE THUNDER

PROMISES
ABOUT WORRY

Why do you worry about clothes?
Look at how the lilies in the field grow.
They don't work or make clothes for themselves.
But I tell you that even Solomon with his riches
was not dressed as beautifully as one of these flowers.
God clothes the grass in the field, which is alive today
but tomorrow is thrown into the fire.
So you can be even more sure that
God will clothe you.

MATTHEW 6:28–30

Do not worry about anything,
but pray and ask God for everything you need,
always giving thanks.

PHILIPPIANS 4:6

Continue praying, keeping alert,
and always thanking God.

COLOSSIANS 4:2

WORRY

Worry changes nothing. You don't add one day to your life or one bit of life to your day by worrying. Your anxiety earns you heartburn, nothing more. Regarding the things about which we fret:

- 40 percent never happen
- 30 percent regard unchangeable deeds of the past
- 12 percent focus on the opinions of others that cannot be controlled
- 10 percent center on personal health, which only worsens as we worry about it
- 8 percent concern real problems that we can influence

Ninety-two percent of our worries are needless! Not only is worry irrelevant, doing nothing; worry is irreverent, distrusting God.

COME THIRSTY

PROMISES ABOUT SUFFERING

Those who go to God Most High for safety
will be protected by the Almighty.
I will say to the LORD,
"You are my place of safety and protection.
You are my God and I trust you."

PSALM 91:1–2

LORD, even when I have trouble all around me,
you will keep me alive.
When my enemies are angry,
you will reach down and save me by your power.

PSALM 138:7

I leave you peace; my peace I give you.
I do not give it to you as the world does.
So don't let your hearts be troubled or afraid.

JOHN 14:27

SUFFERING

There is a window in your heart through which you can see God. Once upon a time that window was clear. Your view of God was crisp. You could see God as vividly as you could see a gentle valley or hillside.

Then, suddenly, the window cracked. A pebble broke the window. A pebble of pain.

And suddenly God was not so easy to see. The view that had been so crisp had changed.

You were puzzled. God wouldn't allow something like this to happen, would he?

When you can't see him, trust him. . . . Jesus is closer than you've ever dreamed.

IN THE EYE OF THE STORM

PROMISES ABOUT OPTIMISM

We thank God! He gives us the victory
through our Lord Jesus Christ.

1 CORINTHIANS 15:57

God did not give us a spirit that makes us afraid
but a spirit of power and love and self-control.

2 TIMOTHY 1:7

The LORD says, "I will make you wise
and show you where to go.
I will guide you and watch over you."

PSALM 32:8

Depend on the LORD;
Trust him, and he will take care of you.

PSALM 35:7

OPTIMISM

Bedtime is a bad time for kids. No child understands the logic of going to bed while there is energy left in the body or hours left in the day.

My children are no exception. A few years ago, after many objections and countless groans, the girls were finally in their gowns, in their beds, and on their pillows. I slipped into the room to give them a final kiss. Andrea, the five-year-old was still awake, just barely, but awake. After I kissed her, she lifted her eyelids on final time and said, "I can't wait until I wake up."

Oh, for the attitude of a five-year-old! That simple uncluttered passion for living that can't wait for tomorrow. A philosophy of life that reads, "Play hard, laugh hard, and leave the worries to your father." A bottomless well of optimism flooded by a perpetual spring of faith.

AND THE ANGELS WERE SILENT

73

*The wisdom that comes from God is first
of all pure, then peaceful, gentle, and easy to please.
This wisdom is always ready to help those who
are troubled and to do good for others.
It is always fair and honest.*

JAMES 3:17

*When you are angry, do not sin, and be sure
to stop being angry before the end of the day.
Do not give the devil a way to defeat you.*

EPHESIANS 4:26–27

*My dear brothers and sisters,
always be willing to listen and slow to speak.
Do not become angry easily, because anger will not
help you live the right kind of life God wants.*

JAMES 1:19–20

ANGER

Anger. It's a peculiar yet predictable emotion. It begins as a drop of water. An irritant. A frustration. Nothing big, just an aggravation. Someone gets your parking place. A waitress is slow and you are in a hurry. Drip. Drip. Drip.

Yet, get enough of these seemingly innocent drops of anger and before long you've got a bucket full of rage. Walking revenge. Blind bitterness. Unharnessed hatred. . . .

Now, is that any way to live? What good has hatred ever brought? What hope has anger ever created?

We can't deny that our anger exists. How do we harness it? A good option is found in Luke 23:34. Here, Jesus speaks about the mob that killed him. "Father, forgive them, because they don't know what they are doing."

NO WONDER THEY CALL HIM THE SAVIOR

PROMISES ABOUT
DISAPPOINTMENT

Do not lose the courage you had in the past,
which has a great reward. You must hold on,
so you can do what God wants and receive
what he has promised.

HEBREWS 10:35–36

We must not become tired of doing good.
We will receive our harvest of eternal life
at the right time if we do not give up.

GALATIANS 6:9

God began doing a good work in you,
and I am sure he will continue it until
it is finished when Jesus Christ comes again.

PHILIPPIANS 1:6

LORD, even when I have trouble all around me,
you will keep me alive.
When my enemies are angry,
you will reach down and save me by your power.

PSALM 138:7

DISAPPOINTMENT

Have you taken your disappointments to God?
You've shared them with your neighbor, your
relatives, your friends. But have you taken them to
God? James says, "Anyone who is having troubles
should pray" (James 5:13).

Before you go anywhere else with your
disappointments, go to God.

Maybe you don't want to trouble God with your
hurts. After all, he's got famines and pestilence and
wars; he won't care about my little struggles, you think.
Why don't you let him decide that? He cared enough
about a wedding to provide the wine. He cared
enough about Peter's tax payment to give him a coin.
He cared enough about the woman at the well to give
her answers. "He cares about you" (1 Peter 5:7).

TRAVELING LIGHT

PROMISES
About
PERSONAL
RELATIONSHIPS

PROMISES ABOUT
LOYAL FRIENDSHIP

I urge you now to live the life to which
God called you. Always be humble, gentle, and patient,
accepting each other in love. You are joined together
with peace through the Spirit, so make every effort
to continue together in this way.

EPHESIANS 4:1-3

Love each other deeply, because love will
cause many sins to be forgiven. Open your homes
to each other, without complaining. Each of you has
received a gift to use to serve others. Be good servants
of God' various gifts of grace.

1 PETER 4:8-10

Be sure that no one pays back wrong for wrong,
but always try to do what is
good for each other and for all people.

1 THESSALONIANS 5:15

LOYAL FRIENDSHIP

What do you do with a friend? You stick by him.

Maybe that is why John is the only one of the twelve who was at the cross. He came to say good-bye. By his own admission he hadn't quite put the pieces together yet. But that didn't really matter. As far as he was concerned, his closest friend was in trouble and he came to help.

"Can you take care of my mother?"

Of course. That's what friends are for.

John teaches us that the strongest relationship with Christ may not necessarily be a complicated one. He teaches us that the greatest webs of loyalty are spun, not with airtight theologies or foolproof philosophies, but with friendships; stubborn, selfless, joyful friendships.

NO WONDER THEY CALL HIM THE SAVIOR

PROMISES ABOUT
RESOLVING RESENTMENT

So why do you judge your brothers or sisters in Christ?
And why do you think you are better than they are?
We will all stand before God to be judged. . . .

The LORD hates evil thoughts
but is pleased with kind words.

PROVERBS 15:26

Whoever forgives someone's sin makes a friend,
but gossiping about the sin breaks up friendships.

PROVERBS 17:9

All of you should be in agreement,
understanding each other, loving each other as family,
being kind and humble. Do not do wrong to repay a wrong,
and do not insult to repay an insult. But repay with
a blessing, because you yourselves were called
to do this so that you might receive a blessing.

1 PETER 3:8–9

RESOLVING RESENTMENT

Resentment is the cocaine of the emotions. It causes our blood to pump and our energy level to rise. But, also like cocaine, it demands increasingly large and more frequent dosages. There is a dangerous point at which anger ceases to be an emotion and becomes a driving force. A person bent on revenge moves unknowingly further and further away from being able to forgive, for to be without the anger is to be without a source of energy.

Hatred is the rabid dog that turns on its owner.

Revenge is the raging fire that consumes the arsonist.

Bitterness is the trap that snares the hunter.

And mercy is the choice that can set them all free.

THE APPLAUSE OF HEAVEN

PROMISES ABOUT
PRAYING FOR OTHERS

*I tell you that if two of you on earth agree
about something and pray for it, it will be done for you
by my Father in heaven. This is true because if two or three
people come together in my name, I am there with them.*

MATTHEW 18:19–20

*Confess your sins to each other
and pray for each other so God can heal you.
When a believing person prays, great things happen.*

JAMES 5:16

*Do good to those who hate you,
bless those who curse you, pray for those
who are cruel to you.*

LUKE 6:27–28

*Brothers and sisters, I beg you to help me in my work
by praying to God for me. Do this because of our Lord Jesus
and the love that the Holy Spirit gives us.*

ROMANS 15:30

PRAYING FOR OTHERS

How did Jesus endure the terror of the crucifixion? He went first to the Father with his fears. He modeled the words of Psalm 56:3: "When I am afraid, I will trust you."

Do the same with yours. Don't avoid life's Gardens of Gethsemane. Enter them. Just don't enter them alone. And while there, be honest. Pounding the ground is permitted. Tears are allowed. And if you sweat blood, you won't be the first. Do what Jesus did; open your heart.

And be specific. Jesus was. "Take this cup," he prayed. Give God the number of the flight. Tell him the length of the speech. Share the details of the job transfer. He has plenty of time. He also has plenty of compassion.

TRAVELING LIGHT

PROMISES
ABOUT CONFLICT

If someone does wrong to you,
do not pay him back by doing wrong to him.
Try to do what everyone thinks is right.
Do your best to live in peace with everyone.

ROMANS 12:17–18

Those who work to bring peace are happy,
because God will call them his children.

MATTHEW 5:9

Agree with each other, and live in peace.
Then the God of love and peace will be with you.

2 CORINTHIANS 13:11

CONFLICT

Want to see a miracle? Plant a word of love heartdeep in a person's life. Nurture it with a smile and a prayer, and watch what happens.

An employee gets a compliment. A wife receives a bouquet of flowers. . . .

Sowing seeds of peace is like sowing beans. You don't know why it works; you just know it does. Seeds are planted, and topsoils of hurt are shoved away. . . .

Jesus modeled this. We don't see him settling many disputes or negotiating conflicts. But we do see him cultivating inward harmony through acts of love. . . .

He built bridges by healing hurts. He prevented conflict by touching the interior. He cultivated harmony by sowing seeds of peace in fertile hearts.

THE APPLAUSE OF HEAVEN

PROMISES ABOUT
GODLY PARENTING

Know and believe today that the LORD is God.
He is God in heaven above and on the earth below.
There is no other god! Obey his laws and commands that
I am giving you today so that things will go well for you
and your children. Then you will live a long time in the land
that the LORD your God is giving to you forever.

DEUTERONOMY 4:39–40

Correct your children, and you will be proud;
they will give you satisfaction.

PROVERBS 29:17

All your children will be taught by the LORD,
and they will have much peace.

ISAIAH 54:13

Fathers, do not make your children angry,
but raise them with the
training and teaching of the Lord.

EPHESIANS 6:4

GODLY PARENTING

When our oldest daughter, Jenna, was two, I lost her in a department store. One minute she was at my side and the next she was gone. I panicked. All of a sudden only one thing mattered—I had to find my daughter. Shopping was forgotten. The list of things I came to get was unimportant. I yelled her name. What people thought didn't matter. For a few minutes, every ounce of energy had one goal—to find my lost child. (I did, by the way. She was hiding behind some jackets!)

No price is too high for a parent to pay to redeem his child. No energy is too great. No effort too demanding. A parent will go to any length to find his or her own.

So will God.

Mark it down. God's greatest creation is not the flung stars or the gorged canyons; it's his eternal plan to reach his children.

AND THE ANGELS WERE SILENT

PROMISES ABOUT
VALUING OTHERS

My brothers and sisters, God called you to be free,
but do not use your freedom as an excuse to do
what pleases your sinful self. Serve each other with love.
The whole law is made complete in this one command:
"Love your neighbor as you love yourself."

GALATIANS 5:13–14

Let us think about each other and
help each other to show love and do good deeds.

HEBREWS 10:24

In the same way, younger people should be willing
to be under older people. And all
of you should be very humble with each other.
"God is against the proud,
but he gives grace to the humble."

1 PETER 5:5

VALUING OTHERS

God sees us with the eyes of a Father. He sees our defects, errors, and blemishes. But he also sees our value.

What did Jesus know that enabled him to do what he did?

Here's part of the answer. He knew the value of people. He knew that each human being is a treasure. And because he did, people were not a source of stress but a source of joy.

In the Eye of the Storm

PROMISES ABOUT
SERVING OTHERS

If there are poor among you,
in one of the towns of the land the LORD your God
is giving you, do not be selfish or greedy toward them.
But give freely to them, and freely lend them
whatever they need.

DEUTERONOMY 15:7–8

Religion that God accepts as pure and
without fault is this: caring for orphans or widows
who need help, and keeping yourself free from
the world's evil influence.

JAMES 1:27

A brother or sister in Christ might need clothes or food.
If you say to that person "God be with you!
I hope you stay warm and get plenty to eat,"
but you do not give what that person needs,
your words are worth nothing.

JAMES 2:15–16

SERVING OTHERS

There are times when we . . . are called to love,
expecting nothing in return. Times when we are
called to give money to people who will never say
thanks, to forgive those who won't forgive us, to
come early and stay late when no one else notices.

Service prompted by duty. This is the call
of discipleship.

Mary and Mary knew a task had to be done—
Jesus' body had to be prepared for burial. Peter didn't
offer to do it. Andrew didn't volunteer. . . . So the
two Marys decide to do it. . . .

Mary and Mary thought they were alone.
They weren't. They thought their journey was
unnoticed. They were wrong. God knew. He was
watching them walk up the mountain. He was
measuring their steps. He was smiling at their hearts
and thrilled at their devotion.

He Still Moves Stones

PROMISES ABOUT
FORGIVING OTHERS

When you are praying, if you are angry
with someone, forgive him so that
your Father in heaven will also forgive your sins.

MARK 11:25

God has chosen you and made you his holy people.
He loves you. So always do these things:
Show mercy to others, be kind, humble, gentle, and patient.
Get along with each other, and forgive each other.
If someone does wrong to you, forgive that person
because the Lord forgave you.

COLOSSIANS 3:12–13

Be kind and loving to each other,
and forgive each other just as God
forgave you in Christ.

EPHESIANS 4:32

FORGIVING OTHERS

Bitterness is its own prison.

The sides are slippery with resentment. A floor of muddy anger stills the feet. The stench of betrayal fills the air and stings the eyes. A cloud of self-pity blocks the view of the tiny exit above.

Step in and look at the prisoners. Victims are chained to the walls. Victims of betrayal. Victims of abuse.

The dungeon, deep and dark, is beckoning you to enter. . . . You can, you know. You've experienced enough hurt. . . .

You can choose, like many, to chain yourself to your hurt. . . . Or you can choose, like some, to put away your hurts before they become hates. . . .

How does God deal with your bitter heart? He reminds you that what you have is more important than what you don't have. You still have your relationship with God. No one can take that.

HE STILL MOVES STONES

PROMISES ABOUT
FAMILY PARTINGS

Jesus said to him,
"The foxes have holes to live in,
and the birds have nests,
but the Son of Man has no place
to rest his head."

MATTHEW 8:20

My true brother and sister and mother
are those who do what God wants.

MARK 3:35

All those who have left houses, brothers, sisters, father,
mother, children, or farms to follow me will get much more
than they left, and they will have life forever.

MATTHEW 19:29

FAMILY PARTINGS

It seems that *good-bye* is a word all too prevalent in the Christian's vocabulary. Missionaries know it well. Those who send them know it, too. The doctor who leaves the city to work in the jungle hospital has said it. Those who feed the hungry, those who teach the lost, all know the word *good-bye*.

Airports. Luggage. Embraces. Taillights. "Wave to grandma." Tears. Bus terminals. Ship docks. "Good-bye, Daddy." Tight throats. Ticket counters. Misty eyes. "Write me!"

Question: What kind of God would give you families and then ask you to leave them? What kind of God would give you friends and then ask you to say good-bye?

Answer: A God who knows that we are only pilgrims and that eternity is so close that any "Good-bye" is in reality a "See you tomorrow."

No Wonder They Call Him the Savior

PROMISES ABOUT
COMPASSION

But I say to you, love your enemies.
Pray for those who hurt you. If you do this,
you will be true children of your Father in heaven.

MATTHEW 5:44-45

If someone in your group does something wrong,
you who are spiritual should go to that person and gently help
make him right again. But be careful, because you might be
tempted to sin, too. By helping each other with your troubles,
you truly obey the law of Christ. If anyone thinks he is
important when he really is not, he is only fooling himself.

GALATIANS 6:1-3

This is how we know what real love is:
Jesus gave his life for us.
So we should give our lives for our brothers and sisters.
Suppose someone has enough to live and sees
a brother or sister in need, but does not help. Then God's
love is not living in that person. My children,
we should love people not only with words and talk,
but by our actions and true caring.

1 JOHN 3:16-18

COMPASSION

Picture a battleground strewn with wounded bodies, and you see Bethesda. Imagine a nursing home overcrowded and understaffed, and you see the pool. Call to mind the orphans in Bangladesh or the abandoned in New Delhi, and you will see what people saw when they passed Bethesda. As they passed, what did they hear? An endless wave of groans. What did they witness? A field of faceless need. What did they do? Most walked past, ignoring the people.

But not Jesus. . . .

He is alone. . . .The people need him—so he's there. Can you picture it? Jesus walking among the suffering. . . .

Little do they know that God is walking slowly, stepping carefully between the beggars and the blind.

HE STILL MOVES STONES

PROMISES
of
WISDOM

PROMISES ABOUT
SELF-WORTH

People should think of us as servants of Christ,
the ones God has trusted with his secrets. Now in this way
those who are trusted with something valuable must show
they are worthy of that trust. As for myself, I do not care if
I am judged by you or by any human court. I do not even
judge myself. . . .The Lord is the One who judges me.

1 CORINTHIANS 4:1–4

Do not let anyone treat you as if you are unimportant
because you are young. Instead, be an
example to the believers with your words, your actions,
your love, your faith, and your pure life.

1 TIMOTHY 4:12

You have begun to live the new life, in which you
are being made new and are becoming like the One
who made you. This new life brings you the true knowledge
of God. In the new life there is no difference between Greeks
and Jews . . . or those who are foreigners, or Scythians.
There is no difference between slaves and free people.
But Christ is in all believers, and Christ
is all that is important.

COLOSSIANS 3:10–11

SELF-WORTH

"He has made perfect forever those who are being made holy," . . .

Underline the word *perfect*. Note that the word is not *better*. Not *improving*. Not *on the upswing*. God doesn't improve; he perfects. He doesn't enhance; he completes. . . .

Now I realize that there's a sense in which we're imperfect. We still err. We still stumble. We still do exactly what we don't want to do. And that part of us is, according to the verse, "being made holy."

But when it comes to our position before God, we're perfect. When he sees each of us, he sees one who has been made perfect through the One who is perfect—Jesus Christ.

IN THE EYE OF THE STORM

PROMISES ABOUT
ACCEPTING GOD'S LOVE

Christ had no sin,
but God made him become sin so that in Christ
we could become right with God.

2 CORINTHIANS 5:21

Love never ends.

1 CORINTHIANS 13:8

The Father has loved us so much that
we are called children of God.
And we really are his children.

1 JOHN 3:1

We know the love that God has for us,
and we trust that love.

1 JOHN 4:16

ACCEPTING GOD'S LOVE

It's time to let God's love cover all things in your life. All secrets. All hurts. All hours of evil, minutes of worry.

The mornings you awoke in the bed of a stranger? His love will cover that. The years you peddled prejudice and pride? His love will cover that. Every promise broken, drug taken, penny stolen. Every cross word, cuss word, and harsh word. His love covers all things.

Let it. Discover along with the psalmist: "He . . . loads me with love and mercy" (Psalm 103:4). Picture a giant dump truck full of love. There you are behind it. God lifts the bed until the love starts to slide. Slowly at first, then down, down, down until you are hidden, buried, covered in his love.

A LOVE WORTH GIVING

PROMISES ABOUT
FINDING REST

Remember to keep the Sabbath holy.
Work and get everything done during six days each week,
but the seventh day is a day of rest to honor the LORD
your God. On that day no one may do any work. . . .
The reason is that in six days the LORD made everything—
the sky, the earth, the sea, and everything in them.
On the seventh day he rested. So the LORD blessed
the Sabbath day and made it holy.

EXODUS 20:8–11

God will do what is right.
He will give trouble to those who trouble you.
And he will give rest to you who are troubled. . .

2 THESSALONIANS 1:6–7

We who have believed are
able to enter and have God's rest.

HEBREWS 4:3A

FINDING REST

Time has skyrocketed in value. The value of any commmodity depends on its scarcity. And time that once was abundant now is going to the highest bidder. . . .

When I was ten years old, my mother enrolled me in piano lessons. . . . Spending thirty minutes every afternoon tethered to a piano bench was a torture just one level away from swallowing broken glass. . . .

Some of the music, though, I learned to enjoy. I hammered the staccatos. I belabored the crescendos. . . . But there was one instruction in the music I could never obey to my teacher's satisfaction. The rest. The zigzagged command to do nothing. What sense does that make? Why sit at the piano and pause when you can pound?

"Because," my teacher patiently explained, "music is always sweeter after a rest."

It didn't make sense to me at age ten. But now, years later, the words ring with wisdom—divine wisdom.

THE APPLAUSE OF HEAVEN

PROMISES ABOUT
SETTING PRIORITIES

*Respecting the LORD and not being proud
will bring you wealth, honor, and life.*

PROVERBS 22:4

*In every way be an example of doing good deeds.
When you teach, do it with honesty and seriousness.
Speak the truth so that you cannot be criticized. . . .
Grace teaches us to live now in a wise and right way
and in a way that shows we serve God. We should live like that
while we wait for our great hope and the coming of the
glory of our Great God and Savior Jesus Christ.*

TITUS 2:7–8, 12–13

*God is fair; he will not forget the work you did
and the love you showed for him by helping his people.
And he will remember that you are still helping them.
We want each of you to go on with the same hard work
all your lives so you will surely get what you hope for.*

HEBREWS 6:10–11

SETTING PRIORITIES

There is only so much sand in the hourglass. Who gets it?

You know what I'm talking about, don't you? . . .

"The PTA needs a new treasurer. With your background and experience and talent and wisdom and love for kids and degree in accounting, YOU are the perfect one for the job!" . . .

It's tug-of-war, and you are the rope. . . .

"Blessed are the meek," Jesus said. The word meek does not mean weak. It means focused. It is a word used to describe a domesticated stallion. Power under control. Strength with a direction. . . .

Blessed are those who recognize their God-given responsibilities. Blessed are those who acknowledge that there is only one God and have quit applying for his position. Blessed are those who know what on earth they are on earth to do and set themselves about the business of doing it.

IN THE EYE OF THE STORM

PROMISES ABOUT
CORRECTING MISTAKES

If you hide your sins, you will not succeed.
If you confess and reject them, you will receive mercy.

PROVERBS 28:13

If you listen to correction to improve your life,
you will live among the wise.
Those who refuse correction hate themselves,
but those who accept correction gain understanding.
Respect for the LORD will teach you wisdom.
If you want to be honored, you must be humble.

PROVERBS 15:31-33

In the kingdom of God . . . the important things
are living right with God, peace, and joy in the Holy Spirit.
Anyone who serves Christ by living this way is pleasing
God and will be accepted by other people. So let us try
to do what makes peace and helps one another.

ROMANS 14:17-19

CORRECTING MISTAKES

Do-it-yourself Christianity is not much encouragement to the done in and worn out.

Self-sanctification holds little hope for the addict. . . .

At some point we need more than good advice; we need help. Somewhere on this journey home we realize that a fifty-fifty proposition is too little. We need more. . . .

We need help. Help from the inside out. . . . Not near us. Not above us. Not around us. But in us. In the part of us we don't even know. In the heart no one else has seen. In the hidden recesses of our being dwells, not an angel, not a philosophy, not a genie, but God.

WHEN GOD WHISPERS YOUR NAME

PROMISES ABOUT
BEING USED BY GOD

But if any of you needs wisdom,
you should ask God for it. He is generous and enjoys
giving to all people, so he will give you wisdom.

JAMES 1:5

If we confess our sins, he will forgive our sins,
because we can trust God to do what is right.
He will cleanse us from all the wrongs we have done.

1 JOHN 1:9

But in all these things we have full victory
through God who showed his love for us.

ROMANS 8:37

BEING USED BY GOD

God used (and uses!) people to change the world. People! Not saints or superhumans or geniuses, but people. Crooks, creeps, lovers, and liars—he uses them all. And what they may lack in perfection, God makes up for in love.

If you ever wonder how God can use you to make a difference in your world, just look at those he has already used and take heart. Look at the forgiveness found in those open arms and take courage.

And, by the way, never were those arms opened so wide as they were on the Roman cross. One arm extending back into history and the other reaching into the future. An embrace of forgiveness offered for anyone who'll come. A hen gathering her chicks. A father receiving his own. A redeemer redeeming the world.

NO WONDER THEY CALL HIM THE SAVIOR

PROMISES ABOUT
DEALING WITH THE PAST

We know that in everything God works
for the good of those who love him.
They are the people he called,
because that was his plan.

ROMANS 8:28

Why am I so sad?
Why am I so upset?
I should put my hope in God
and keep praising him,
my Savior and my God.

PSALM 43:5

I know that I have not yet reached that goal,
but there is one thing I always do. Forgetting the past
and straining toward what is ahead, I keep trying to
reach the goal and get the prize for which God called
me through Christ to the life above.

PHILIPPIANS 3:13–14

DEALING WITH
THE PAST

Perhaps your childhood memories bring more hurt than inspiration. The voices of your past cursed you, belittled you, ignored you. At the time, you thought such treatment was typical. Now you see it isn't.

And now you find yourself trying to explain your past. Do you rise above the past and make a difference? Or do you remain controlled by the past and make excuses?

Think about this. Spiritual life comes from the Spirit! Your parents may have given you genes, but God gives you grace. Your parents may be responsible for your body, but God has taken charge of your soul. You may get your looks from your mother, but you get eternity from your Father, your heavenly Father. And God is willing to give you what your family didn't.

WHEN GOD WHISPERS YOUR NAME

PROMISES ABOUT
DARING TO DREAM

When the LORD All-Powerful makes a plan,
no one can stop it.

ISAIAH 14:27

"My thoughts are not like your thoughts.
Your ways are not like my ways.
Just as the heavens are higher than the earth,
so are my ways higher than your ways
and my thoughts higher than your thoughts.
So you will go out with joy
and be led out in peace."

ISAIAH 55:8, 12

Don't be afraid, because I am your God.
I will make you strong and will help you;
I will support you with my right hand that saves you. . . .
I am the LORD your God, who holds your right hand,
and I tell you, "Don't be afraid. I will help you."

ISAIAH 41:10

DARING TO DREAM

God always rejoices when we dare to dream. In fact, we are much like God when we dream. The Master exults in newness. He delights in stretching the old. He wrote the book on making the impossible possible.

Examples? Check the Book.

Eighty-year-old shepherds don't usually play chicken with Pharoahs . . . but don't tell that to Moses.

Teenage shepherds don't normally have showdowns with giants . . . but don't tell that to David.

Night-shift shepherds don't usually get to hear angels sing and see God in a stable . . . but don't tell that to the Bethlehem bunch.

And for sure don't tell that to God.

AND THE ANGELS WERE SILENT

PROMISES ABOUT
MAKING RIGHT CHOICES

Trust the LORD with all your heart,
and don't depend on your own understanding.
Remember the LORD in all you do,
and he will give you success.

PROVERBS 3:5–6

You were taught to leave your old self—
to stop living the evil way you lived before.
That old self becomes worse,
because people are fooled by the evil things
they want to do. But you were taught to be made new
in your hearts, to become a new person.
That new person is made to be like God—
made to be truly good and holy.

EPHESIANS 4:22–24

Now that you are obedient children of God
do not live as you did in the past.
You did not understand,
so you did the evil things you wanted.
But be holy in all you do, just as God,
the One who called you, is holy.

1 PETER 1:14–15

MAKING
RIGHT CHOICES

I have something against the lying voices that noise our world. You've heard them. They tell you to swap your integrity for a new sale. To barter your convictions for an easy deal. To exchange your devotion for a quick thrill.

They whisper. They woo. They taunt. They tantalize. They flirt. They flatter. "Go ahead, its OK." "Don't worry, no one will know."

The world rams at your door; Jesus taps at your door. The voices scream for your allegiance; Jesus softly and tenderly requests it. The world promises flashy pleasure; Jesus promises a quiet dinner . . . with God.

Which voice do you hear?

IN THE EYE OF THE STORM

119

PROMISES
About
JESUS

PROMISES ABOUT
JESUS, THE SAVIOR

God loved the world so much that he gave
his one and only Son so that whoever believes in him
may not be lost, but have eternal life. God did not send
his Son into the world to judge the world guilty,
but to save the world through him.

JOHN 3:16–17

If you use your mouth to say, "Jesus is Lord,"
and if you believe in your heart that God raised Jesus
from the dead, you will be saved.

ROMANS 10:9

We have seen and can testify that the Father
sent his Son to be the Savior of the world.

1 JOHN 4:14

JESUS, THE SAVIOR

He looked around the hill and foresaw a scene. Three figures hung on three crosses. Arms spread. Heads fallen forward. They moaned with the wind.

Men clad in soldiers' garb sat on the ground near the trio.

Men clad in religion stood off to one side. . . . Arrogant, cocky.

Women clad in sorrow huddled at the foot of the hill. . . . Faces tear streaked.

All heaven stood to fight. All nature rose to rescue. All eternity poised to protect. But the Creator gave no command.

"It must be done . . . ," he said, and withdrew.

The angel spoke again. "It would be less painful . . ."

The Creator interrupted softly. "But it wouldn't be love."

IN THE EYE OF THE STORM

PROMISES ABOUT JESUS, OUR LORD

So God raised him to the highest place.
God made his name greater than every other name
so that every knee will bow to the name of Jesus—
everyone in heaven, on earth, and under the earth.
And everyone will confess that Jesus Christ is Lord
and bring glory to God the Father.

PHILIPPIANS 2:9-11

We do not live or die for ourselves.
If we live, we are living for the Lord, and if we die,
we are dying for the Lord. So living or dying,
we belong to the Lord.

ROMANS 14:7-8

For the wages of sin is death,
but the gift of God is eternal life in
Christ Jesus our Lord.

ROMANS 6:23

JESUS, OUR LORD

The bad is perplexingly close to the good. The just is frighteningly near to the unfair. And life? Life is always a clock's tick away from death. And evil? Evil is paradoxically close to goodness.

It's this eerie inconsistency that keeps all of us, to one degree or another, living our lives on the edge of our chairs.

Yet, it was in this inconsistency that God had his finest hour. Never did the obscene come so close to the holy as it did on Calvary. Never did the good in the world so intertwine with the bad as it did on the cross. Never did what is right involve itself so intimately with what is wrong, as it did when Jesus was suspended between heaven and earth.

God on a cross. Humanity at its worst. Divinity at its best.

No Wonder They Call Him the Savior

PROMISES THAT JESUS IS RISEN

Jesus said to her, "I am the resurrection and the life.
Those who believe in me will have life even if they die.
And everyone who lives and believes in me will never die."

JOHN 11:25–26A

But Christ has truly been raised
from the dead—the first one and proof that those
who sleep in death will also be raised.

1 CORINTHIANS 15:20

God raised the Lord Jesus from the dead,
and we know that God will also raise us with Jesus.
God will bring us together with you,
and we will stand before him.

2 CORINTHIANS 4:14

We believe that Jesus died and that he rose again.
So, because of him, God will raise with Jesus
those who have died.

1 THESSALONIANS 4:14

JESUS IS RISEN

Those who saw Jesus—really saw Him—knew there was something different. At His touch blind beggars saw. At His command crippled legs walked. At His embrace empty lives filled with vision.

He fed thousands with one basket. He stilled a storm with one command. He raised the dead with one proclamation. He changed lives with one request. He rerouted the history of the world with one life, lived in one country, was born in one manger, and died on one hill.

He became a man so we could trust him. He became a sacrifice so we could know him. And he defeated death so we could follow him.

What man can't do, God does.

AND THE ANGELS WERE SILENT

PROMISES THAT
JESUS CARES FOR US

*The LORD searches all the earth for people
who have given themselves completely to him.
He wants to make them strong. . . .*

2 CHRONICLES 16:9

*But, LORD, you are my shield,
my wonderful God who gives me courage.*

PSALM 3:3

*The Lord is faithful and will give you
strength and will protect you from the Evil One.*

2 THESSALONIANS 3:3

*I love the LORD,
because he listens to my prayers for help.
He paid attention to me,
so I will call to him for help as long as I live.*

PSALM 116:1

JESUS CARES FOR US

The shepherd knows his sheep. He calls them by name. When we see a crowd, we see exactly that, a crowd. . . . We see people, not persons, but people. A herd of humans. A flock of faces. That's what we see.

But not so with the Shepherd. To him every face is different. Every face is a story. Every face is a child. Every child has a name. . . .

The shepherd knows his sheep. He knows each one by name. The Shepherd knows you. He knows your name. And he will never forget it.

WHEN GOD WHISPERS YOUR NAME

PROMISES ABOUT
JESUS, OUR HOPE

*Praise be to the God and Father of
our Lord Jesus Christ. In God's great mercy he has
caused us to be born again into a living hope,
because Jesus Christ rose from the dead.*

1 PETER 1:3

*Now I am right with God, not because
I followed the law, but because I believed in Christ.
God uses my faith to make me right with him.
I want to know Christ and the power that
raised him from the dead. . . . Then I have hope
that I myself will be raised from the dead.*

PHILIPPIANS 3:9–11

*These two things cannot change: God cannot lie
when he makes a promise, and he cannot lie
when he makes an oath. These things encourage us
who came to God for safety. They give us strength
to hold on to the hope we have been given. We have this
hope as an anchor for the soul, sure and strong.*

HEBREWS 6:18–19

JESUS, OUR HOPE

The one to whom we pray knows our feelings. He knows temptation. He has felt discouraged. He has been hungry and sleepy and tired. He knows what we feel like when the alarm clock goes off. He knows what we feel like when our children want different things at the same time. He nods in understanding when we pray in anger. He is touched when we tell him there is more to do than can ever be done. He smiles when we confess our weariness.

He, too, was human. He wants us to know that he, too, knew the drone of the humdrum and the weariness that comes with long days. He wants us to remember that our trailblazer didn't wear bulletproof vests or rubber gloves or an impenetrable suit of armor. No, he pioneered our salvation through the world that you and I face daily. He became flesh and dwelt among us.

NO WONDER THEY CALL HIM THE SAVIOR

Promises about Jesus, our Unchanging God

Before the mountains were born
And before you created the earth and the world
You are God.

PSALM 90:2

You are all around me—in front and in back—
And have put your hand on me.
Your knowledge is amazing to me;
It is more than I can understand.

PSALM 139:5–6

God said to Moses, "I AM WHO I AM."

EXODUS 3:14

JESUS, OUR UNCHANGING GOD

Relationships change. Health changes. The weather changes. But the God who ruled the earth last night is the same God who rules it today. Same convictions. Same plan. Same mood. Same love. He never changes. You can no more alter God than a pebble can alter the rhythm of the Pacific. He is our middle C. A still point in a turning world. Don't we need a still point? Don't we need an unchanging shepherd?

Counselors can comfort you in the storm, but you need a God who can still the storm. Friends can hold your hand at your deathbed, but you need a Yahweh who has defeated the grave. Philosophers can debate the meaning of life, but you need a Lord who can declare the meaning of life.

TRAVELING LIGHT

PROMISES ABOUT JESUS, THE GOOD SHEPHERD

The LORD is my shepherd;
I have everything I need.
He lets me rest in green pastures.
He leads me to calm water.
He gives me new strength.
He leads me on paths that are right
for the good of his name.

PSALM 23:1–3

I am the good shepherd.
The good shepherd gives his life for the sheep.
I am the good shepherd. I know my sheep,
as the Father knows me. And my sheep know me,
as I know the Father. I give my life for the sheep.

JOHN 10:11, 14

God raised from the dead our Lord Jesus,
the Great Shepherd of the sheep, because of
the blood of his death. His blood began the eternal
agreement that God made with his people.

HEBREWS 13:20–21

JESUS, THE GOOD SHEPHERD

Sheep aren't smart. They tend to wander into running creeks for water, then their wool grows heavy and they drown. They need a shepherd to lead them to "calm water" (Psalm 23:2). They have no natural defense—no claws, no horns, no fangs. They are helpless. Sheep need a shepherd with a "rod and . . . walking stick" (Psalm 23:4) to protect them. They have no sense of direction. They need someone to lead them "on paths that are right" (Psalm 23:3).

So do we. We, too, tend to be swept away by waters we should have avoided. We have no defense against the evil lion who prowls about seeking who he might devour. We, too, get lost.

We need a shepherd. We need a shepherd to care for us and to guide us. And we have one. One who knows us by name.

A GENTLE THUNDER

PROMISES ABOUT JESUS, OUR BURDEN-BEARER

Give your worries to the LORD,
and he will take care of you.
He will never let good people down.

PSALM 55:22

But [the Lord] said to me,
"My grace is enough for you. When you are weak,
my power is made perfect in you." . . . For this reason
I am happy when I have weaknesses, insults, hard times,
sufferings, and all kinds of troubles for Christ.
Because when I am weak, then I am truly strong.

2 CORINTHIANS 12:9–10

Since Christ suffered while he was in his body,
strengthen yourselves with the same way of thinking
Christ had. . . . Strengthen yourselves so that
you will live here on earth doing what God wants,
not the evil things people want.

1 PETER 4:1–2

JESUS, OUR BURDEN-BEARER

When it comes to healing our spiritual condition, we don't have a chance. We might as well be told to pole-vault the moon. We don't have what it takes to be healed. Our only hope is that God will do for us what he did for the man at Bethesda—that he will step out of the temple and step into our ward of hurt and helplessness.

Which is exactly what he has done. . . .

I wish we would take Jesus at his word. . . .

When he says we're forgiven, let's unload the guilt.

When he says we're valuable, let's believe him.

When he says we're eternal, let's bury our fear.

When he says we're provided for, let's stop worrying.

God's efforts are strongest when our efforts are useless.

HE STILL MOVES STONES

PROMISES ABOUT JESUS, OUR SECURITY

[He] is strong and can help you not to fall.
He can bring you before his glory without any
wrong in you and can give you great joy.

JUDE 24

But the Lord is faithful and will give you
strength and will protect you from the Evil One.

2 THESSALONIANS 3:3

May our Lord Jesus Christ himself and God our Father
encourage you and strengthen you in every good thing you
do and say. God loved us, and through his grace he gave us
a good hope and encouragement that continues forever.

2 THESSALONIANS 2:16, 17

Now we hope for the blessings God has for his children.
These blessings, which cannot be destroyed or be spoiled
or lose their beauty, are kept in heaven for you.
God's power protects you through your faith until
salvation is shown to you at the end of time.

1 PETER 1:4–5

JESUS, OUR SECURITY

You and I are on a great climb. The wall is high, and the stakes are higher. You took your first step the day you confessed Christ as the Son of God. He gave you his harness—the Holy Spirit. In your hands he placed a rope—his Word.

Your first steps were confident and strong, but with the journey came weariness, and with the height came fear. You lost your footing. You lost your focus. You lost your grip, and you fell. For a moment, which seemed like forever, you tumbled wildly. Out of control. Out of self-control. Disoriented. Dislodged. Falling.

But then the rope tightened, and the tumble ceased. You hung in the harness and found it to be strong. You grasped the rope and found it to be true. And though you can't see your guide, you know him. You know he is strong. You know he is able to keep you from falling.

A GENTLE THUNDER

PROMISES ABOUT JESUS,
THE GLORY OF ETERNITY

Look, Jesus is coming with the clouds,
and everyone will see him. . . .
And all peoples of the earth will
cry loudly because of him.
Yes, this will happen!

REVELATION 1:7

Always be ready, because you don't know the day
your Lord will come. . . . . Because the Son of Man will
come at a time you don't expect him.

MATTHEW 25:42, 44

Just as everyone must die once and be judged,
so Christ was offered as a sacrifice one time to take away
the sins of many people. And he will come
a second time, not to offer himself for sin, but to bring
salvation to those who are waiting for him.

HEBREWS 9:27–28

JESUS, THE GLORY OF ETERNITY

Every person who has ever lived will be present at that final gathering. Every heart that has ever beat. Every mouth that has ever spoken. On that day you will be surrounded by a sea of people. Rich, poor. Famous, unknown. Kings, bums. Brilliant, demented. All will be present. And all will be looking in one direction. All will be looking at Him—the Son of Man. Wrapped in splendor. Shot through with radiance.

You won't look at anyone else. No side-glances to see what others are wearing. No whispers about new jewelry or comments about who is present. At this, the greatest gathering in history, you will have eyes for only one.

AND THE ANGELS WERE SILENT

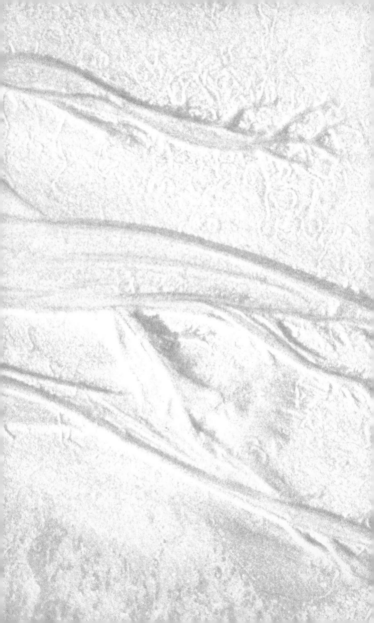

PROMISES
When You Have
SPECIAL NEEDS

PROMISES ABOUT BEING RIGHT BEFORE GOD

Love never hurts a neighbor,
so loving is obeying all the law. Do this because
we live in an important time. It is now time for you
to wake up from your sleep, because our salvation
is nearer now than when we first believed.

ROMANS 13:10–11

Now respect the LORD and serve him
fully and sincerely. . . . Serve the LORD.
But if you don't want to serve the LORD, you must
choose for yourselves today whom you will serve.

JOSHUA 24:14–15

Jesus has the power of God, by which he has given us
everything we need to live and to serve God. We have
these things because we know him. Jesus called us
by his glory and goodness. Through these he gave us
the very great and precious promises. With these gifts
you can share in being like God, and the world
will not ruin you with its evil desires.

2 PETER 1:3–4

BEING RIGHT
BEFORE GOD

We are thirsty.

Not thirsty for fame, possessions, passion, or romance. We've drunk from those pools. They are salt water in the desert. They don't quench—they kill.

"Blessed are those who hunger and thirst for righteousness. . . ."

Righteousness. That's it. That's what we are thirsty for. We're thirsty for a clean conscience. We crave a clean slate. We yearn for a fresh start. We pray for a hand that will enter the dark cavern of our world and do for us the one thing we can't do for ourselves— make us right again.

THE APPLAUSE OF HEAVEN

PROMISES ABOUT FACING DEATH

*Yea, though I walk through the valley of the
shadow of death, I will fear no evil;
for You are with me;
Your rod and Your staff, they comfort me.*

PSALM 23:4, NKJV

*We all must die, and everyone living
should think about this.*

ECCLESIASTES 7:2

*Teach us how short our lives really are
so that we may be wise.*

PSALM 90:12

*All the days planned for me were written
in your book before I was one day old.*

PSALM 138:16

FACING DEATH

Don't face death without facing God. Don't even speak of death without speaking to God. He and he alone can guide you through the valley. Others may speculate or aspire, but only God knows the way to get you home. And only God is committed to getting you there safely.

Jesus said: "There are many rooms in my Father's house; I would not tell you this if it were not true. I am going there to prepare a place for you. After I go and prepare a place for you, I will come back and take you to be with me so that you may be where I am" (John 14:2–3).

He pledges to take us home. He does not delegate this task. He may send missionaries to teach you, angels to protect you, teachers to guide you, singers to inspire you, and physicians to heal you, but he sends no one to take you. He reserves this job for himself.

TRAVELING LIGHT

PROMISES ABOUT
FEELING OVERWHELMED

LORD, answer me because your love is so good.
Because of your great kindness, turn to me.
Do not hide from me, your servant.
I am in trouble. Hurry to help me!
Come near and save me;
rescue me from my enemies.

PSALM 69:16–18

I love the LORD,
because he listens to my prayers for help.
He paid attention to me,
so I will call to him for help as long as I live.

PSALM 116:1–2

I have good plans for you, not plans to hurt you.
I will give you hope and a good future.
Then you will call my name.
You will come to me and pray to me, and I
will listen to you. You will search for me. And when you
search for me with all your heart, you will find me!

JEREMIAH 29:11–13

FEELING OVERWHELMED

Ever feel the wheels of your life racing faster and faster as you speed past the people you love? Could you use a reminder on how to slow it all down?

Read what Jesus did during the last Sabbath of his life. Start in the Gospel of Matthew. Didn't find anything? Try Mark. . . . Nothing there either? Strange. What about Luke? What does Luke say? Not a reference to the day? Not a word about it? Well, try John. Surely John mentions the Sabbath. He doesn't? No reference? Hmmmm. Looks like Jesus was quiet that day.

"Wait a minute. That's it?" That's it.

"You mean with all those apostles to train and people to teach, he took a day to rest and worship?" Apparently so.

AND THE ANGELS WERE SILENT

PROMISES ABOUT
GOD'S ANSWERS
TO OUR PRAYERS

Ask, and God will give to you.
Search, and you will find. Knock, and the door
will open for you. Yes, everyone who asks will receive.
Everyone who searches will find. And everyone
who knocks will have the door opened.

MATTHEW 7:7-8

Without faith no one can please God.
Anyone who comes to God must believe that he is real
and that he rewards those who truly want to find him.

HEBREWS 11:6

And this is the boldness we have in God's presence:
that if we ask God for anything that agrees with what
he wants, he hears us. If we know he hears us every time
we ask him, we know we have what we ask from him.

1 JOHN 5:14-15

GOD'S ANSWERS TO OUR PRAYERS

"Go back and report to John what you hear and see: The blind receive sight, the lame walk . . . and the good news is preached to the poor."

This was Jesus' answer to John's agonized query from the dungeon of doubt: "Are you the one who was to come, or should we expect someone else?"

We don't know how John received Jesus' message but we can imagine. I like to think of a slight smile coming over his lips as he heard what his Master said. For now he understood. It wasn't that Jesus was silent; it was that John had been listening for the wrong answer. John had been listening for an answer to his earthly problems, while Jesus was busy resolving his heavenly ones.

That's worth remembering the next time you hear the silence of God.

THE APPLAUSE OF HEAVEN

PROMISES ABOUT
LONGING FOR HEAVEN

I have no one in heaven but you;
I want nothing on earth besides you.
My body and my mind may become weak,
but God is my strength.
He is mine forever.

PSALM 73:25–26

There are many rooms in my Father's house;
I would not tell you this if it were not true.
I am going there to prepare a place for you.
I go and prepare a place for you,
I will come back and take you
to be with me so that you may be where I am.

JOHN 14:2–3

No one has ever seen this,
and no one has ever heard about it.
No one has ever imagined
what God has prepared for those who love him.

1 CORINTHIANS 2:9

LONGING
FOR HEAVEN

The only ultimate disaster that can befall us, I have come to realize, is to feel ourselves to be home on earth. As long as we are aliens, we cannot forget our true homeland.

Unhappiness on earth cultivates a hunger for heaven. By gracing us with a deep dissatisfaction, God holds our attention. The only tragedy, then, is to be satisfied prematurely. To settle for earth.

We are not happy here because we are not supposed to be happy here. We are "like foreigners and strangers in this world" (1 Peter 2:11).

And you will never be completely happy on earth simply because you were not made for earth. Oh, you will have moments of joy. You will catch glimpses of light. You will know moments or even days of peace. But they simply do not compare with the happiness that lies ahead.

WHEN GOD WHISPERS YOUR NAME

PROMISES ABOUT STRUGGLING WITH WORLDLINESS

*Think only about the things in heaven,
not the things on earth. Your old sinful self has died,
and your new life is kept with Christ in God.*

COLOSSIANS 3:2–3

*You should know that loving the world
is the same as hating God. Anyone who wants to
be a friend of the world becomes God's enemy.*

JAMES 4:4

*Do not love the world or the things in the world.
If you love the world, the love of the Father is not in you.
These are the ways of the world: wanting to please
our sinful selves, wanting the sinful things we see,
and being too proud of what we have. None of these
come from the Father, but all of them come from the world.
The world and everything that people want in it
are passing away, but the person who does
what God wants lives forever.*

1 JOHN 2:15–17

STRUGGLING WITH WORLDLINESS

John the Baptist would never get hired today. No church would touch him. He was a public relations disaster. He "wore clothes made from camel's hair, had a leather belt around his waist, and ate locusts and wild honey" (Mark 1:6). Who would want to look at a guy like that every Sunday?

His message was as rough as his dress: a no-nonsense, bare-fisted challenge to repent because God was on his way.

John the Baptist set himself apart for one task, to be a voice of Christ. Everything about John centered on his purpose. His dress. His diet. His actions. His demands.

You don't have to be like the world to have an impact on the world. You don't have to lower yourself down to their level to lift them up to your level. Holiness doesn't seek to be odd. Holiness seeks to be like God.

A GENTLE THUNDER

INSPIRATIONAL PROMISES
ABOUT GROWING OLD

Even when you are old, I will be the same.
Even when your hair has turned gray,
I will take care of you.
I made you and will take care of you.
I will carry you and save you.

ISAIAH 46:4

I was young, and now I am old,
but I have never seen good people left helpless
or their children begging for food.

PSALM 37:25

God, you have taught me since I was young.
To this day I tell about the miracles you do.
Even though I am old and gray,
do not leave me, God.
I will tell the children about your power;
I will tell those who live after me about your might.

PSALM 71:17–18

GROWING OLD

Just when the truth about life sinks in, Jesus takes us by the hand and dares us not to sweep the facts under the rug but to confront them with him at our side.

Aging? A necessary process to pass on to a better world.

Death? Merely a brief passage, a tunnel.

There, was that so bad?

Funerals, divorces, illnesses, and stays in the hospital—you can't lie about life at such times. Maybe that's why he's always present at such moments.

The next time you find yourself alone in a dark alley facing the undeniables of life, don't turn up the TV and pretend they aren't there. Instead, stand still, whisper his name, and listen. He is nearer than you think.

GOD CAME NEAR

PROMISES ABOUT
STRIVING FOR POWER

*Do not fool yourselves. If you think you are
wise in this world, you should become a fool
so that you can become truly wise, because the wisdom
of this world is foolishness with God.*

1 CORINTHIANS 3:18–19

*Where jealousy and selfishness are, there will be
confusion and every kind of evil. But the wisdom that
comes from God is first of all pure, then peaceful, gentle,
and easy to please. This wisdom is always ready
to help those who are troubled and to do good for others.
It is always fair and honest.*

JAMES 3:16–17

*All of you should be very humble with each other.
God is against the proud, but he gives grace to the humble.
Be humble under God's powerful hand so he will
lift you up when the right time comes.*

1 PETER 5:5–6

STRIVING
FOR POWER

The push for power has come to shove. And most of us are either pushing or being pushed.

I might point out the difference between a passion for excellence and a passion for power. The desire for excellence is a gift of God, much needed in society. It is characterized by respect for quality and a yearning to use God's gifts in a way that pleases him.

But there is a canyon of difference between doing your best to glorify God and doing whatever it takes to glorify yourself. The quest for excellence is a mark of maturity. The quest for power is childish.

A thousand years from now, will it matter what title the world gave you? No, but it will make a literal hell of a difference whose child you are.

THE APPLAUSE OF HEAVEN

PROMISES ABOUT
FEELING INSECURE

You made my whole being;
you formed me in my mother's body.
I praise you because you made me
in an amazing and wonderful way.
What you have done is wonderful.
I know this very well.

PSALM 139:13-14

Two sparrows cost only a penny,
but not even one of them can die without your Father's
knowing it. God even knows how many hairs
are on your head. So don't be afraid. You are
worth much more than many sparrows.

MATTHEW 10:29-31

You are God's children whom he loves,
so try to be like him. Live a life of love just as
Christ loved us and gave himself for us as a
sweet-smelling offering and sacrifice to God.

EPHESIANS 5:1-2

FEELING INSECURE

Antonio Stradivari was a seventeenth-century violin maker whose name in its Latin form, Stradivarius, has become synonymous with excellence. He once said that to make a violin less than his best would be to rob God, who could not make Antonio Stradivari's violins without Antonio.

He was right. God could not make Stradivarius violins without Antonio Stradivari. Certain gifts were given to that craftsman that no other violin maker possessed.

In the same vein, there are certain things you can do that no one else can. Perhaps it is parenting, or constructing houses, or encouraging the discouraged. There are things that only you can do, and you are alive to do them. In the great orchestra we call life, you have an instrument and a song, and you owe it to God to play them both sublimely.

THE APPLAUSE OF HEAVEN

PROMISES ABOUT TRYING TO EARN SALVATION

*Since we have been made right with God by our faith,
we have peace with God. This happened through our
Lord Jesus Christ, who has brought us into that blessing
of God's grace that we now enjoy. And we are happy
because of the hope we have of sharing God's glory.*

ROMANS 5:1–2

*The wicked should stop doing wrong,
and they should stop their evil thoughts.
They should return to the Lord
so he may have mercy on them.
They should come to our God,
because he will freely forgive them.*

ISAIAH 55:7

*This is what God told us:
God has given us eternal life, and this life is in his Son.
Whoever has the Son has life,
but whoever does not have the Son of God
does not have life.*

1 JOHN 5:11–12

TRYING TO EARN SALVATION

Love goes the distance . . . and Christ traveled from limitless eternity to be confined by time in order to become one of us. He didn't have to. He could have given up. At any step along the way he could have called it quits.

When he saw the size of the womb, he could have stopped.

When he saw how tiny his hand would be, how soft his voice would be, how hungry his tummy would be, he could have stopped. At the first whiff of the stinky stable, at the first gust of cold air. The first time he scraped his knee or blew his nose or tasted burnt bagels, he could have turned and walked out.

At any point Jesus could have said, "That's it! That's enough! I'm going home." But he didn't.

He didn't, because he is love.

A LOVE WORTH GIVING

163

PROMISES ABOUT GOD'S PURPOSE FOR YOUR LIFE

The LORD says, "My thoughts are not like your thoughts.
Your ways are not like my ways. Just as the heavens
are higher than the earth,
so are my ways higher than your ways
and my thoughts higher than your thoughts."

ISAIAH 55:8−9

Don't worry and say, "What will we eat?" or
"What will we drink?" or "What will we wear?"
The people who don't know God keep trying to get
these things, and your Father in heaven knows
you need them. The thing you should want most is
God's kingdom and doing what God wants.
Then all these other things you need will be given to you.

MATTHEW 6:31−33

If we are not faithful, he will still be faithful,
because he cannot be false to himself. But God's strong
foundation continues to stand. These words are written
on the seal: "The Lord knows those who belong to him,"
and "Everyone who wants to belong to the Lord
must stop doing wrong."

2 TIMOTHY 2:13, 19

GOD'S PURPOSE FOR YOUR LIFE

It's easy to thank God when he does what we want. But God doesn't always do what we want. Ask Job.

His empire collapsed, his children were killed, and what was a healthy body became a rage of boils. From whence came this torrent? From whence will come any help?

Job goes straight to God and pleads his case. His head hurts. His body hurts. His heart hurts.

And God answers. Not with answers but with questions. An ocean of questions. . . .

After several dozen questions . . . Job is left on the beach drenched and wide-eyed, . . . He has gotten the point. What is it?

The point is this: God owes no one anything. No reasons. No explanations. Nothing. If he gave them, we couldn't understand them.

God is God. He knows what he is doing.

THE INSPIRATIONAL STUDY BIBLE

PROMISES

of

ASSURANCE

PROMISES THAT
GOD MEETS OUR NEEDS

The power of the wicked will be broken,
but the LORD supports those who do right.
The LORD watches over the lives of the innocent,
and their reward will last forever.
They will not be ashamed when trouble comes.
They will be full in times of hunger.

PSALM 37:17–19

All that the Father has is mine. . . .
I tell you the truth, my Father will
give you anything you ask for in my name.
Until now you have not asked for anything in my name.
Ask and you will receive, so that your joy
will be the fullest possible joy.

JOHN 16:15, 23–24

My God will use his wonderful riches in
Christ Jesus to give you everything you need.

PHILIPPIANS 4:19

GOD MEETS OUR NEEDS

God's faithfulness has never depended on the faithfulness of his children. He is faithful even when we aren't. When we lack courage, he doesn't. He has made a history out of using people in spite of people.

Need an example? The feeding of the five thousand. It's the only miracle, aside from those of the final week, recorded in all four Gospels. Why did all four writers think it worth repeating? . . . Perhaps they wanted to show how God doesn't give up even when his people do. . . .

When the disciples didn't pray, Jesus prayed.
When the disciples didn't see God, Jesus sought God.
When the disciples were weak, Jesus was strong.
When the disciples had no faith, Jesus had faith.

I simply think God is greater than our weakness.

A Gentle Thunder

PROMISES THAT GOD
WANTS YOU
TO BELONG TO HIM

My whole being, praise the LORD
and do not forget all his kindnesses.
He forgives all my sins
and heals all my diseases.
He saves my life from the grave
and loads me with love and mercy.

PSALM 103:2–4

The LORD your God is with you;
the mighty One will save you.
He will rejoice over you.
You will rest in his love;
he will sing and be joyful about you.

ZEPHANIAH 3:17

The important thing is obeying God's commands.
You all were bought at a great price,
so do not becomes slaves of people.

1 CORINTHIANS 7:19, 23

GOD WANTS YOU TO BELONG TO HIM

For all its peculiarities and unevenness, the Bible has a simple story. God made man. Man rejected God. God won't give up until he wins him back.

God will whisper. He will shout. He will touch and tug. He will take away our burdens; he'll even take away our blessings. If there are a thousand steps between us and him, he will take all but one. But he will leave the final one for us. The choice is ours.

Please understand. His goal is not to make you happy. His goal is to make you his. His goal is not to get you what you want; it is to get you what you need.

A GENTLE THUNDER

PROMISES ABOUT
GOD'S CONSTANT LOVE

God, you are my God.
I search for you.
I thirst for you
like someone in a dry, empty land
where there is no water.
Because your love is better than life,
I will praise you.

PSALM 63:1, 3

LORD, you are kind and forgiving
and have great love for those who call to you.

PSALM 86:5

Where God's love is, there is no fear,
because God's perfect love drives out fear.
It is punishment that makes a person fear,
so love is not made perfect in the person who fears.
We love because God first loved us.

1 JOHN 4:18–19

GOD'S CONSTANT LOVE

"God is love" (1 John 4:16). One word into that passage reveals the supreme surprise of God's love—it has nothing to do with you. Others love you because of you, because your dimples dip when you smile or your rhetoric charms when you flirt. Some people love you because of you. Not God. He loves you because he is he. He loves you because he decides to. Self-generated, uncaused, and spontaneous, his constant-level love depends on his choice to give it.

You don't influence God's love. You can't impact the treeness of a tree, the skyness of the sky, or the rockness of a rock. Nor can you affect the love of God. If your actions altered his devotion, then God would not be love; indeed, he would be human, for this is human love.

COME THIRSTY

PROMISES ABOUT
GOD'S INVITATIONS

"Come to me, all of you who
are tired and have heavy loads,
and I will give you rest."

MATTHEW 11:28

"Come, let us talk about these things.
Though your sins are like scarlet,
They can be as white as snow.
Though your sins are deep red,
They can be white like wool."

ISAIAH 1:18

"Let anyone who is thirsty come to me and drink.
If anyone believes in me,
rivers of living water will flow out
from that person's heart."

JOHN 7:37–38

GOD ISSUES INVITATIONS

You can't read about God without finding him issuing invitations. He invited Eve to marry Adam, the animals to enter the ark, David to be king, Israel to leave bondage, Nehemiah to rebuild Jerusalem. God is an inviting God. He invited Mary to birth his Son, the disciples to fish for men, the adulteress woman to start over, and Thomas to touch his wounds. God is the King who prepares the palace, sets the table, and invites his subjects to come in. . . .

God is a God who invites. God is a God who calls. God is a God who opens the door and waves his hand pointing pilgrims to a full table.

His invitation is not just for a meal, however, it is for life. An invitation to come into his kingdom and take up residence in a tearless, graveless, painless world. Who can come? Whoever wishes.

AND THE ANGELS WERE SILENT

PROMISES THAT
GOD IS SOVEREIGN

Our God is in heaven.
He does what he pleases.

I have always been God.
No one can save people from my power;
when I do something, no one can change it.

ISAIAH 43:13

When I plan something, it happens.
What I want to do, I will do.

ISAIAH 46:10

[God] is the One who makes everything agree
with what he decides and wants.

EPHESIANS 1:11

GOD IS SOVEREIGN

Can you say this about God?

I know God knows what's best.

I know I don't.

I know he cares.

If yes, then you're scoring high marks in the classroom of sovereignty. This important biblical phrase defines itself. Zero in on the middle portion of the term. See the word within the word? Sove-*reign*-ty. To confess the sovereignty of God is to acknowledge the reign of God, his regal authority and veto power over everything that happens. To embrace God's sovereignty is to drink from the well of his lordship. You look to the Captain and resolve: he knows what's best.

COME THIRSTY

PROMISES THAT
GOD EXALTS HUMILITY

Whoever makes himself great will be made humble.
Whoever makes himself humble will be made great.

MATTHEW 23:12

Always be humble, gentle, and patient,
accepting each other in love. You are joined together
with peace through the Spirit, so make every effort
to continue together in this way.

EPHESIANS 4:2

God is against the proud,
but he gives grace to the humble.

JAMES 4:6

Then [Jesus] said, "I tell you the truth,
you must change and become like little children.
Otherwise, you will never enter the kingdom of heaven.
The greatest person in the kingdom of heaven is the one
who makes himself humble like this child."

MATTHEW 18:3–4

GOD EXALTS HUMILITY

Is Jesus not our example? Content to be known as a carpenter. Happy to be mistaken for the gardener. He served his followers by washing their feet. He serves us by doing the same. Each morning he gifts us with beauty. Each Sunday he calls us to his table. Each moment he dwells in our hearts. And does he not speak of the day when he as "the master will dress himself to serve and tell the servants to sit at the table, and he will serve them" (Luke 12:37)?

If Jesus is so willing to honor us, can we not do the same for others? Make people a priority. Accept your part in his plan. Be quick to share the applause. And, most of all, regard others as more important than yourself.

A LOVE WORTH GIVING

PROMISES THAT
GOD BLESSES ENDURANCE

We must not become tired of doing good.
We will receive our harvest of eternal life at the
right time if we do not give up.

GALATIANS 6:9

My brothers and sisters,
when you have many kinds of troubles,
you should be full of joy,
because you know that these troubles test your faith,
and this will give you patience.

JAMES 1:2–3

Those people who keep their faith
until the end will be saved.

MATTHEW 10:22

GOD BLESSES ENDURANCE

Are you close to quitting? Please don't do it. Are you discouraged as a parent? Hang in there. Are you weary with doing good? Do just a little more. Are you pessimistic about your job? Roll up your sleeves and go at it again. No communication in your marriage? Give it one more shot. Can't resist temptation? Accept God's forgiveness and go one more round. Is your day framed with sorrow and disappointment? Are your tomorrows turning into nevers? Is hope a forgotten word?

Remember, a finisher is not one with no wounds or weariness. Quite to the contrary, he, like the boxer, is scarred and bloody.

The Land of Promise, says Jesus, awaits those who endure. It is not just for those who make the victory laps or drink champagne. No sir. The Land of Promise is for those who simply remain to the end.

No Wonder They Call Him the Savior

PROMISES THAT
GOD HONORS INTEGRITY

A wise person will understand what to do,
but a foolish person is dishonest.
Fools don't care if they sin,
but honest people work at being right.

PROVERBS 14:8-9

If people please God, God will give
them wisdom, knowledge, and joy.
But sinners will get only the work of gathering
and storing wealth that they will have to give
to the ones who please God. So all their
work is useless, like chasing the wind.

ECCLESIASTES 2:26

Dear friends, you are like foreigners
and strangers in this world. I beg you to
avoid the evil things your bodies want to do
that fight against your soul.

1 PETER 2:11

GOD HONORS INTEGRITY

Only the holy will see God. Holiness is a prerequisite to heaven. Perfection is a requirement for eternity. We wish it weren't so. We act like it isn't so. We act like those who are "decent" will see God. We suggest that those who try hard will see God. We act as if we're good if we never do anything too bad. And that goodness is enough to qualify us for heaven.

Sounds right to us, but it doesn't sound right to God. And he sets the standard. And the standard is high. "You must be perfect, just as your Father in heaven is perfect" (Matthew 5:48).

You see, in God's plan, God is the standard for perfection. We don't compare ourselves to others; they are just as fouled up as we are. The goal is to be like him; anything less is inadequate.

HE STILL MOVES STONES

PROMISES
About the
CHRISTIAN LIFE

PROMISES ABOUT SIN

*Sin came into the world because of
what one man did, and with sin came death.
This is why everyone must die—because
everyone sinned. One man disobeyed God, and
many became sinners. In the same way, one man
obeyed God, and many will be made right.*

ROMANS 5:12, 19

*Christ had no sin, but God made
him become sin so that in Christ we
could become right with God.*

2 CORINTHIANS 5:21

*Christ himself suffered for sins once.
He was not guilty, but he suffered for those
who are guilty to bring you to God.
His body was killed, but he was
made alive in the spirit.*

1 PETER 3:18

SIN

It wasn't the Romans who nailed Jesus to the cross. It wasn't spikes that held Jesus to the cross. What held him to that cross was his conviction that it was necessary that he become sin—that he who is pure become sin and that the wrath of God be poured down, not upon the creation, but upon the Creator.

When the one who knew no sin became sin for us, when the sinless one was covered with all the sins of all the world, God didn't call his army of angels to save him. He didn't, because he knew he would rather give up his Son than give up on us.

Regardless of what you've done it's not too late. Regardless of how far you've fallen, it's not too late. It doesn't matter how low the mistake is, it's not too late to dig down, pull out that mistake and then let it go—and be free.

What makes a Christian a Christian is not perfection but forgiveness.

WALKING WITH THE SAVIOR

PROMISES ABOUT SALVATION

All have sinned and are not good enough
for God's glory, and all need to be
made right with God by his grace,
which is a free gift. They need to be
made free from sin through Jesus Christ.

ROMANS 3:23–24

If anyone does sin,
we have a helper in the presence
of the Father—Jesus Christ, the One
who does what is right. He is the way our sins
are taken away, and not only our sins
but the sins of all people.

1 JOHN 2:1–2

God did not send his Son into the world
to judge the world guilty, but to save the world
through him. People who believe in God's Son
are not judged guilty. Those who believe in the Son
have eternal life, but those who do not obey the Son
will never have life. God's anger stays on them.

JOHN 3:17, 36

SALVATION

One of the reference points of London is the Charing Cross. It is near the geographical center of the city and serves as a navigational tool for those confused by the streets.

A little girl was lost in the great city. A policeman found her. Between sobs and tears, she explained she didn't know her way home. He asked her if she knew her address. She didn't. He asked her phone number; she didn't know that either. But when he asked her what she knew, suddenly her face lit up.

"I know the Cross," she said. "Show me the Cross and I can find my way home from there."

So can you. Keep a clear vision of the cross on your horizon and you can find your way home.

AND THE ANGELS WERE SILENT

PROMISES ABOUT
REPENTANCE

*Then I confessed my sins to you
and didn't hide my guilt.
I said, "I will confess my sins to the LORD,"
and you forgave my guilt.*

PSALM 32:5

*Change your hearts and lives and be baptized,
each one of you, in the name of Jesus Christ for
the forgiveness of your sins. And you will
receive the gift of the Holy Spirit.*

ACTS 2:38

*I tell you there is more joy in heaven
over one sinner who changes his heart and life,
than over ninety-nine good people
who don't need to change.*

LUKE 15:7

REPENTANCE

"If we confess our sins . . ." The biggest word in Scriptures just might be that two letter one, *if.* For confessing sins—admitting failure—is exactly what prisoners of pride refuse to do.

"Me a sinner? Oh sure, I get rowdy every so often, but I'm a pretty good ol' boy."

"Listen, I'm just as good as the next guy. I pay my taxes. . . ."

Justification. Rationalization. Comparison. . . . They sound good. They sound familiar. They even sound American. But in the kingdom, they sound hollow. . . .

When you get to the point of sorrow for your sins, when you admit that you have no other option . . . then cast all your cares on him for he is waiting.

THE APPLAUSE OF HEAVEN

PROMISES ABOUT
ETERNAL LIFE

I tell you the truth,
whoever believes has eternal life.

JOHN 6:47

You have been born again,
and this new life did not come from something that dies,
but from something that cannot die.
You were born again through God's living message
that continues forever.

1 PETER 1:23

Everyone must die once and be judged.

HEBREWS 9:27

To choose life is to love the LORD your God,
obey him, and stay close to him.
He is your life. . . .

DEUTERONOMY 30:20

ETERNAL LIFE

Our task on earth is singular—to choose our eternal home. You can afford many wrong choices in life. You can choose the wrong career and survive, the wrong city and survive, the wrong house and survive. You can even choose the wrong mate and survive. But there is one choice that must be made correctly and that is your eternal destiny.

We are free either to love God or not. He invites us to love Him. He urges us to love Him. He came that we might love Him. But, in the end, the choice is yours and mine. To take that choice from each of us, for Him to force us to love Him, would be less than love. . . .

He leaves the choice to us.

AND THE ANGELS WERE SILENT

PROMISES ABOUT SANCTIFICATION

*If people's thinking is controlled by the sinful self,
there is death. But if their thinking is controlled by
the Spirit, there is life and peace. When people's thinking
is controlled by the sinful self, they are against God,
because they refuse to obey God's law and really are not
even able to obey God's law. Those people who are
ruled by their sinful selves cannot please God.*

ROMANS 8:6–8

*We all show the Lord's glory, and we are being changed
to be like him. This change in us brings ever greater glory,
which comes from the Lord, who is the Spirit.*

2 CORINTHIANS 3:18

*Surely you know that the people who do wrong
will not inherit God's kingdom. In the past,
some of you were like that, but you were washed clean.
You were made holy, and you were made right with
God in the name of the Lord Jesus Christ
and in the Spirit of our God.*

1 CORINTHIANS 6:9, 11

SANCTIFICATION

I wonder if Jesus doesn't muster up a slight smile as he sees his lost sheep come straggling into the fold—the beaten, broken, dirty sheep who stands at the door looking up at the Shepherd asking, "Can I come in? I don't deserve it, but is there room in your kingdom for one more?" The Shepherd looks down at the sheep and says, "Come in, this is your home."

Salvation is the process that's done, that's secure, that no one can take away from you. Sanctification is the lifelong process of being changed from one degree of glory to the next, growing in Christ, putting away the old, taking on the new.

The Psalmist David would tell us that those who have been redeemed will say so! If we're not saying so, perhaps it's because we've forgotten what it is like to be redeemed. Let the redeemed of the earth say so!

WALKING WITH THE SAVIOR

195

PROMISES ABOUT
GOD'S PLAN

"I love you people with a love
that will last forever.
That is why I have continued
showing you kindness."

JEREMIAH 31:3

Because of his love and kindness,
he saved them.

ISAIAH 63:9

Brothers and sisters, whom the Lord loves,
God chose you from the beginning to be saved.
So we must always thank God for you.
You are saved by the Spirit that makes you holy
and by your faith in the truth.

2 THESSALONIANS 2:13

GOD'S PLAN

Jesus' death was not the result of a panicking, cosmological engineer. The cross wasn't a tragic surprise. Calvary was not a knee-jerk response to a world plummeting towards destruction. It wasn't a patch-job or a stop-gap measure. The death of the Son of God was anything but an unexpected peril.

No, it was part of a plan. It was a calculated choice. "It was the LORD who decided to crush him and make him suffer." (Isaiah 53:10) The cross was drawn into the original blueprint. It was written into the script. The moment the forbidden fruit touched the lips of Eve, the shadow of a cross appeared on the horizon. And between that moment and the moment the man with the mallet placed the spike against the wrist of God, a master plan was fulfilled.

GOD CAME NEAR

PROMISES ABOUT
LIVING LIKE CHRIST

You are the light that gives light to the world.
A city that is built on a hill cannot be hidden.
And people don't hide a light under a bowl.
They put it on a lampstand so the light shines for all
the people in the house. In the same way,
you should be a light for other people.
Live so that they will see the good things
you do and will praise your Father in Heaven.

MATTHEW 5:14–16

This work must continue until we are all joined
together in the same faith and in the same knowledge of the
Son of God. We must become like a mature person, growing
until we become like Christ and have his perfection.

EPHESIANS 4:13

Anyone who speaks should speak words from God.
Anyone who serves should serve with the strength
God gives so that in everything God will be
praised through Jesus Christ. Power and glory
belong to him forever and ever.

1 PETER 4:11

LIVING LIKE CHRIST

Sacred delight is good news coming through the back door of your heart. It's what you'd always dreamed but never expected.

It is sacred because only God can grant it. It is a delight because it thrills.

It is this sacred delight that Jesus promises in the Sermon on the Mount.

And he promises it to an unlikely crowd:

"The poor in spirit . . . Those who mourn . . .

The meek . . . Those who hunger and thirst . . .

The merciful . . . The pure in heart . . .

The peacemakers . . . The persecuted . . ."

It is to this band of pilgrims that God promises a special blessing. A heavenly joy. A sacred delight.

THE APPLAUSE OF HEAVEN

PROMISES ABOUT
THE BODY OF CHRIST

A person's body is only one thing,
but it has many parts. Though there are many parts
to a body, all those parts make only one body. Christ is
like that also, . . . we were all baptized into one body
through one Spirit. And we were all made
to share in the one Spirit.

1 CORINTHIANS 12:12–13

Let the teaching of Christ live in you richly.
Use all wisdom to teach and instruct each other by
singing psalms, hymns, and spiritual songs with thankfulness
in your hearts to God. Everything you do or say should
be done to obey Jesus your Lord. And in all you do,
give thanks to God the Father through Jesus.

COLOSSIANS 3:16–17

You are a chosen people, royal priests, a holy nation,
a people for God's own possession. You were chosen to tell
the wonderful acts of God, who called you out of
darkness into his wonderful light.

1 PETER 2:9

THE BODY
OF CHRIST

In the third century, St. Cyprian wrote to a friend named Donatus:

This seems a cheerful world, Donatus, when I view it from this fair garden. . . . But if I climbed some great mountain and looked out . . . you know very well what I would see; brigands on the high road, pirates on the seas, in the amphitheaters men murdered to please the applauding crowds. . . .

Yet in the midst of it, I have found a quiet and holy people. . . . They are despised and persecuted, but they care not. They have overcome the world. These people, Donatus, are Christians. . . .

What a compliment! *A quiet and holy people. . . .*

Quiet. . . . Not obnoxious. Not boastful. Not demanding. Just quiet. . . .

Holy. . . . Set apart. Pure. Decent. Honest. Wholesome. . . .

THE STUDY BIBLE

PROMISES ABOUT HEAVEN

The LORD has set his throne in heaven,
and his kingdom rules over everything.

You have this faith and love because of your hope,
and what you hope for is kept safe for you in heaven.
You learned about this hope when you heard the message
the truth, the Good News that was told to you.

COLOSSIANS 1:5–6A

People will insult you and hurt you.
They will lie and say all kinds of evil things you
because you follow me. But when they do,
you will be happy. Rejoice and be glad, because you
have a great reward waiting for you in heaven.

MATTHEW 5:11–12

HEAVEN

"I will live in the house of the LORD forever" (Psalm 23:6).

Where will you live forever? In the house of the Lord. If his house is your "forever house," what does that make this earthly house? You got it! Short-term housing. This is not our home. "Our homeland is in heaven" (Philippians 3:20).

My friends Jeff and Carol just adopted two small children. Christopher, the older, is only three, but he knows the difference between Jeff's house and the foster home from which he came. He tells all visitors, "This is my forever home."

Won't it be great when we can say the same?

TRAVELING LIGHT

203

ACKNOWLEDGMENTS

Grateful acknowledgment is made to the following publishers for permission to reprint this copyrighted material. All copyrights are held by the author, Max Lucado.

Lucado, Max. *The Applause of Heaven* (Nashville: W. Publishing Group, 1990).

———*In the Eye of the Storm* (Nashville: W Publishing Group, 1991).

———*He Still Moves Stones* (Nashville: W Publishing Group, 1993).

———*When God Whispers Your Name* (Nashville: W Publishing Group, 1994)

———*A Gentle Thunder* (Nashville: W Publishing Group, 1995).

Max Lucado, General Editor, *The Inspirational Study Bible* (Nashville: W Publishing Group, 1995)

———*In the Grip of Grace* (Nashville: W. Publishing Group, 1996).

———*Just Like Jesus* (Nashville: W Publishing Group, 1998).

————*He Chose the Nails* (Nashville: W Publishing Group, 2000).

————*Traveling Light* (Nashville: W Publishing Group, 2000).

————*God Came Near* (Nashville: W Publishing Group, 2003).

————*No Wonder They Call Him the Savior* (Nashville: W Publishing Group, 2003).

————*Six Hours One Friday* (Nashville: W Publishing Group, 2003).

————*And the Angels Were Silent* (Nashville: W Publishing Group, 2003).